Revolution
in Science

TIME
LIFE ®
BOOKS

This volume is one of a series that examines
various aspects of computer technology
and the role computers play in modern life.

UNDERSTANDING COMPUTERS

Revolution in Science

BY THE EDITORS OF TIME-LIFE BOOKS

TIME-LIFE BOOKS, ALEXANDRIA, VIRGINIA

Contents

Through the Numbers Barrier

The universe, said the great 17th century Italian scholar Galileo Galilei, is a "grand book written in the language of mathematics." This statement, shocking to the ecclesiastical authorities of his land, epitomized a new approach to scientific inquiry. Breaking with the medieval view that Holy Scripture and church-guided philosophy alone could explain the workings of nature, Galileo and his contemporaries sought truth from close observation of the physical world and rigorous mathematical logic. The result was a bonanza of understanding. All manner of phenomena, from the behavior of planets to the nature of light, began to bare their secrets. Science has been conducted in the same way ever since.

Mathematics itself underwent rapid evolution during the 17th century and afterward. Nonetheless, as scientists probed deeper into the workings of the physical world, their reach sometimes threatened to exceed their grasp. For example, the German astronomer Johannes Kepler, a contemporary of Galileo's, developed a theory—later known as Kepler's laws—that described the orbits of planets in simple mathematical terms. To decipher the planetary pattern, he spent eight years computing the orbit of Mars. At the end of his toil, he confessed, "I was almost driven to madness in considering and calculating this matter."

Today, however, an astronomer can perform equivalent calculations in minutes, thanks to a miracle tool that has wrought a second revolution in science. From the study of stars to the probing of subatomic particles, the physical sciences have become inextricably bound up with the electronic computer, a machine whose facility with the language of mathematics is breathtaking.

Numerical drudgery is only one of the burdens computers shoulder for scientists. These machines now serve in every stage of scientific research. In laboratories or in the field, they control instruments and record and analyze data. When an experiment is complete, computers are often used to express the results as a graphic display of surpassing clarity. They also explore phenomena that are impossible to investigate by direct means: Conditions within the earth, inside a cell or in the perilous vicinity of a black hole can be described in the form of equations—a mathematical model, as it is called—and simulated electronically.

NUMBERS IN THE HEAVENS

The road that led from the age of Galileo to the dawn of the computer era was a long and winding one, and only near the end did scientists begin to sense that something truly extraordinary lay ahead. For most of the journey, the limits of human computational ability grew progressively more frustrating even as the power of mathematics was becoming more evident.

This was particularly true in a discipline that fascinated Galileo—celestial mechanics, the study of the motion of planets and stars. Galileo was an avid astronomer, the first to turn a telescope on the night sky. He used his observa-

tions and his mathematical skills to develop convincing proof of the Copernican theory that the earth and other planets revolve around the sun—a centerpiece of the original Scientific Revolution. Succeeding generations of astronomers found extended calculations to be an essential part of their work, and many of them, like Kepler, devoted several years of their lives to a single project.

Of such computationally intensive tasks, perhaps the most urgent was the production of a type of navigational table that dealt with the moon's position in the sky and enabled a mariner to determine his position at sea. First, the navigator used a sextant to measure the angular distance between the moon and a relatively motionless star—an angle that at any one moment is the same no matter where on the earth's surface the measurement is made. The table, called a lunar ephemeris, correlated star-to-moon angular distances with particular times of the day for every day of the year. Once the navigator had worked out the precise time of day with the aid of the table listings, he could employ additional star sightings and other celestial tables to calculate his longitude—the east-west component of the ship's position.

Achieving accuracy in the lunar ephemeris listings was the problem. To predict the position of the moon with the exactitude needed for navigational tables involved exceedingly complicated mathematics. Isaac Newton, the British genius who worked out the laws governing the moon's motion, confessed that the effort "made his head ache and kept him awake so often that he could think of it no more."

If the only influence acting upon the moon were the gravity of the earth, determining lunar position would be what mathematicians call a two-body problem, a relatively simple exercise. Unfortunately, the orbit of the moon is extremely complex, for it is affected by the gravitational attraction of both the earth and the sun. Additional complexity arises in the form of perturbations—irregularities in the orbit caused by such factors as the slight variations from spherical shape in the earth and the moon.

In 1675, the British government established the Royal Observatory at Greenwich for "the finding out of the longitude of places for perfecting navigation and astronomy." In 1714, after navigational errors had caused a major disaster for the British fleet, a prize in the then-huge amount of £20,000 was offered to anyone who "could discover the longitude at sea." Many of the leading minds of the day attacked the problem. It was not until 1753 that the cartographer Tobias Mayer, using methods of calculation devised by the mathematician Leonhard Euler, developed the first accurate lunar tables; each man received £3,000 from the government. The tables were turned over to the Royal Observatory, where Nevil Maskelyne, fifth Astronomer Royal, incorporated them in the first British *Nautical Almanac*—a volume of tables showing the positions of many celestial bodies for every midnight and noon during 1767. In an updated and revised form, it has been published every year since. Despite the appearance of reliable seagoing chronometers at about the same time the first *Nautical Almanac* was produced, the lunar time-telling method stayed in common use for more than a century. Nautical timepieces were very expensive, and even a navigator who possessed one was likely to take an occasional lunar measurement during a long voyage to check the accuracy of the chronometer.

Unfortunately, for decades after its introduction, the almanac was riddled with errors. The entries were worked out mainly by elderly clergymen, augmenting their pensions with the pittance wages the observatory paid for computational labor. The first edition alone contained more than a thousand errors. After Maskelyne's death in 1811, the quality of the complex calculations deteriorated even further, and the almanacs became dangerously unreliable. Then the pendulum swung back. In 1834, improved calculation techniques involving seven-figure logarithms were introduced. These, along with an upgrading of the computational work force, largely eliminated errors from the tables, but the labor was still sisyphean and mind-numbing. And that was how the situation remained until 1926, when Leslie John Comrie, a 32-year-old New Zealander, was appointed deputy superintendent of the office that produced the *Nautical Almanac*.

As a young man, Comrie served in World War I with the New Zealand Expeditionary Force in France, where he lost a leg. He then entered Cambridge University to seek a doctoral degree in astronomy, and there he undertook a task for the British Astronomical Association that launched his career in the computational side of celestial mechanics. The association, a professional society for astronomers, assigned him the highly abstruse—and purely academic—job of predicting the times various celestial bodies would eclipse or pass behind each other when the earth and sun pass through the plane of the rings of Saturn. It soon became clear that very extensive calculations were involved, and this led to the establishment of a computing section within the association. Comrie's growing skill at organizing such massive numerical work was recognized by his appointment to head the section. His success there led to the position at the Nautical Almanac Office.

BRINGING IN THE MACHINES

By the time Comrie was chosen for the deputy superintendent post in Greenwich in 1926, he had become convinced that mechanical calculating equipment could perform scientific computations more efficiently than humans. The most

advanced was the punched-card calculator, introduced in the 1890s when American inventor Herman Hollerith saved the U.S. Census Bureau from foundering in a sea of demographic data by employing his machines to add up the census figures automatically. About the size of a small office desk, Hollerith's statistical tabulator took its data from cards punched with holes that represented information about the population, such as age, sex and country of origin. The cards were moved over a bath of electrically conductive mercury, with many metal brushes pushing lightly against the tops; wherever there was a hole, a brush would contact the mercury, closing a circuit that caused a counting device to add data to the total. It worked so well that the 1890 census was completed in one third the time that its predecessor had taken. Comrie was determined to introduce updated Holleriths—by then manufactured by IBM—to the task of computing the astronomical tables.

But his crusty personality and the tradition-bound nature of the Nautical Almanac Office made this transition a rough one. While a student at Cambridge, Comrie had spent two months at the office, seeing how it worked. He was unimpressed. The computation methods were nearly a century old, and the calculations were largely assigned to outside workers—retired staff members for the most part. The system operated efficiently enough, but there were no facilities for training new staff and virtually no scope for new ideas. Student though he was, Comrie did not hesitate to recommend reforms to the Astronomer Royal. That eminent civil servant replied that it was not Comrie's role to teach Greenwich its job. Thus when Comrie settled into the job in 1926, he was viewed with a certain coolness and suspicion.

By all accounts, Comrie was difficult to work with—single-minded to the point of fanaticism (an accusation that he took as a compliment), quick to quarrel, tactless and intolerant of faults in others. But these were the traits of a man who sought precision in all things. Comrie's friends, who stressed his many good qualities, were amazed by the care with which he would weigh out the exact amount of salt prescribed for his domestic water softener. Each night before retiring to bed (where he relaxed by reading mathematical texts), he would check his pocket watch against the BBC time signal and then enter the result on a graph of the watch's performance.

In his new post, he acted quickly. Overriding or bypassing his critics, he rented Hollerith tabulators to compute the moon's position at noon and midnight for every day of the year from 1935 to the year 2000. Nearly 100 million figures describing lunar motion were used in the calculations. The solutions were printed over the course of seven months. Comrie himself estimated that the method "increased tenfold the speed with which results can be obtained, and reduced the cost to one quarter of its former amount."

The computations for this latest lunar ephemeris were based on tables of the moon's motion created at Yale University by the British-born astronomer Ernest Brown. In the summer of 1928, Brown visited London and witnessed the mechanical spinning out of his work. Comrie later wrote: "I shall ever remember his ecstasies of rapture as he saw his figures being added at the rate of 20 or 30 a second."

THE WORD SPREADS

When Brown returned to Yale after his visit to England, he discussed Comrie's methods with one of his Ph.D. students, an astronomer and mathematician named Wallace Eckert. Under Brown's influence, Eckert developed what would prove to be a lifelong interest in the calculations involved in celestial mechanics. After receiving his doctorate in 1931, the 29-year-old Eckert took a position at Columbia University in New York as an assistant professor.

Columbia was an ideal place for him to develop his practical interest in computing; the university had a special tie with IBM, by then one of the largest manufacturers of mechanical calculating and tabulating equipment. The relationship began in 1929, when Columbia psychologist Benjamin Wood was casting about for machines that could be used to process the results of standardized psychological tests. With no funds to buy the equipment he wanted, Wood decided to try getting it free from a manufacturer. Granted a brief meeting with Thomas Watson Sr., IBM's chief executive, Wood eloquently explained the benefits that IBM machines could bring not only to his own work but to any academic discipline based on numerical data, from biology to astronomy. So impressed was Watson with Wood's enthusiasm that the meeting stretched long into the afternoon; two days later, a crew of IBM technicians arrived at Columbia with several truckloads of equipment, free of charge. These machines became the core of the Columbia University Statistical Bureau, which provided computing services to social scientists.

Soon after the bureau was established, Eckert visited it and watched the machines at work. "For an astronomer who had been doing computations the hard way," he recalled two decades later, "it was a great experience." He saw an accounting machine printing the results of 150 additions per minute; cards were sorted at the rate of about 20,000 cards an hour. Although he concluded that the equipment in the Statistical Bureau lacked the features needed for astronomical research, he soon learned that IBM was about to put several new, more flexible machines on the market.

Eckert resolved to get some of these machines for Columbia's astronomy department. His vision was of "an automatic scientific computing laboratory where complete intricate astronomical computations could be performed without any reading or writing of figures." A small, retiring man, so soft-spoken that colleagues often had to strain to catch his comments, Eckert proved just as single-minded as Comrie and as persuasive as Wood. In 1933, he too turned to Watson, submitting through Wood a list of the equipment he wanted. After a few weeks of quiet negotiations, the machines were delivered—again, entirely at IBM's expense—to the attic of the building that housed Columbia's observatory. The resulting laboratory, with a beautiful view of the Hudson River, was operational by early 1934.

The machines included a card punch, used to transfer the data of a problem from paper records to punched cards; a verifier, which checked the initial data on the cards against a second keying from the manuscript; a sorter, capable of automatically sorting the cards into groups at the rate of 20,000 cards per hour; a tabulator, which did the actual additions, reading the numbers from 9,000 cards per hour, and which, when equipped with a printing mechanism, could print information from individual cards or give the accumulated totals; and a high-speed reproducer, which transferred information from one card to another at the rate of 6,000 cards per hour.

Pride of place went to a multiplier built to Eckert's specifications at IBM's factory in Endicott, New York, under the supervision of Clair Lake, the top engineer in the company. Fabricated from standard punched-card machine parts, it was the only device of its time that could automatically multiply numbers together. This feat was performed at the rate of 730 cards per hour for eight-digit-by-eight-digit multiplications.

Among the first jobs for the astronomical laboratory was a catalogue of the

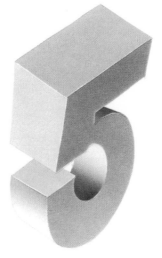

positions of thousands of stars, based on a voluminous photographic record compiled at the Yale University Observatory. A vast number of simple calculations were required to match the locations of stars on flat photographic plates with their spherical coordinates in the sky. The most recent such catalogue had been compiled in 1870, and it had required the joint effort of all the world's principal observatories over the course of a generation. Columbia alone did the new calculations, completing the job in only a few years, at about half the estimated cost of hand computation, and achieving a much higher level of accuracy than the old catalogue.

The success of Eckert's computing facility made it an attraction for other astronomers. By 1937, the demand for its services resulted in the creation of a nonprofit organization—jointly operated by Columbia, IBM and the American Astronomical Society—that performed calculations for astronomers around the world. The modest Eckert gave credit to the generosity of Watson, who was doubtless gratified by the name of the new facility: the Thomas J. Watson Astronomical Computing Bureau.

If the techniques introduced at Columbia made a big splash with astronomers, they produced only a few ripples in the larger realm of science. Eckert did his best to spread the news of his methods: He wrote a book called *Punched Card Methods in Scientific Computation,* which Columbia published and gave away to interested scientists. But not until the onset of World War II did advances in mechanical computing begin to penetrate other scientific domains.

SPEEDING UP WAR WORK

Just three hours after hostilities between Great Britain and Germany began in 1939, Leslie John Comrie received an urgent request from the British War Office to prepare some ballistic tables—charts indicating for gunners the trajectories of artillery shells fired at different angles and under a variety of weather conditions. Comrie, whose run-ins with superiors at the admiralty had led to his resignation in 1936, had formed a company to provide large-scale computation services on a commercial basis. The business operated as efficiently as Comrie could have wished; within 12 days of receiving the War Office request, a pair of 200-page volumes of tables had been compiled, printed, indexed and bound.

About a year later, at the height of the Battle of Britain, the firm tackled the even more difficult problem of locating a radio beacon that the Germans were using to guide their bomb-laden aircraft to British targets. In the wake of each raid, fragmentary and often inaccurate reports from observers were supplied to Comrie's team. After several months of mathematical backtracking, greatly complicated by the incompleteness of the data, the team produced its estimate of the beacon's position. A reconnaissance flight took off immediately, and the well-camouflaged station was discovered within 100 yards of the predicted location.

Meanwhile, on the other side of the Atlantic, Wallace Eckert went into government service as director of the *Nautical Almanac* at the Naval Observatory in Washington. As Comrie had at Greenwich, Eckert found the existing methods of computation deficient. "It was obvious that the war was about to start," he recalled. "The tables were needed more quickly, and additional new tables were required." He arranged to have punched-card machines installed, providing the capacity for computation and table-making on a large scale.

One of the first tasks for the new equipment was to create navigation tables for the ships engaged in a life-and-death struggle with German U-boats in the Atlantic. To fight the submarines effectively, Allied warships protecting convoys needed quick information on the location of an attack. The existing navigation tables generally listed the positions of celestial bodies for one or two times each day. When a ship was attacked, navigators took as much as half an hour to determine their whereabouts and relay their position to escort vessels—an interval that could allow an enemy raider to sink more ships or make good its escape.

Working in secrecy, Eckert, a young supervisor named Jack Belzer and a group of assistants began compiling special nautical almanacs with far more detailed listings. By reducing the mathematics demanded of navigators, the new tables made it possible to calculate positions in as little as a minute on the basis of observations of the sun or stars. Because the added detail required much more computational effort in the creation of the tables, almanacs were compiled only for a 10-degree latitude band over the North Atlantic and only for the specific periods when convoys would be at sea. Since sailing dates might be arranged with only a few days' notice, however, Eckert's team sometimes had just a few hours to make their computations, let alone get the almanacs printed and dispatched to the waiting navigators. At best, Eckert's team was never more than a week ahead of deadlines, and airplanes had to be kept standing by to rush the almanacs to their destinations. But the effort was richly repaid. Within a few weeks of the introduction of the almanacs, shipping losses on the North Atlantic route began to diminish.

HELPING UNSHACKLE THE NUCLEAR GENIE

Comrie and Eckert were only two among a multitude of scientists who turned to war work. The scientific research lab—in fields such as aerodynamics, electronics and chemistry—was a little-documented but absolutely critical front in a conflict fought at ever-higher levels of technology. By far the largest research endeavor was the top-secret Manhattan Project, which, beginning in late 1942, brought hundreds of scientists to Los Alamos, New Mexico, to develop an atomic bomb. By late 1943, the large computation problems involved were beginning to exceed the capacity of the computing equipment, which consisted of slide rules and desk calculators. At one of the project's weekly meetings, physicist Hans Bethe reported a particularly intractable problem: He had developed equations to describe the progress of atomic fission in a variety of potential designs, but the equations were too complicated to solve with the available machines. Dana Mitchell, a professor on leave from Columbia University, was a member of the group who heard Bethe's report. He immediately recalled Eckert's work in astronomy at Columbia, and after some discussion, it was decided to order IBM machines similar to those used at the Astronomical Computing Bureau.

The shroud of secrecy enfolding the project was so complete that even IBM was not allowed to know where the machines were to be used or to send an installation crew. Instead, the Los Alamos team sought out the best IBM maintenance man then serving in the U.S. Army. The technician, John Johnston, was quickly assigned to the project, where he found that the scientists had already set up the equipment, using wiring diagrams as instructions. Congratulating them on their ingenuity (no one outside of IBM had ever successfully assembled one of the machines), Johnston proceeded to sort out some technical problems that had kept them from functioning properly.

In a contest arranged between the hand-computing group and the punched-card machine operation, the new equipment clearly proved its superiority, but the urgency and complexity of the Manhattan Project soon pressed the IBM machines to the limits of their capabilities. A second shift was added to the computer operation, then another, with both working six days a week. Various ways of modifying the equipment to speed up their operation were devised, and in May 1944 more powerful multipliers and machines that could divide were specially commissioned from IBM.

Nevertheless, the mathematical demands of the Manhattan Project overmatched the equipment, demonstrating the fundamental weakness of the punched-card machines in scientific applications. Designed for commercial applications such as payroll work and inventory control, they could handle relatively large amounts of input data and a small amount of calculation on each piece of data. Eckert's astronomical computations were similar. To produce the lunar ephemeris, for example, the machines had performed a relatively short sequence of operations on each of the thousands of entries from the lunar motion tables. Unfortunately, scientific users often dealt with smaller amounts of input data and long chains of calculation, so jobs had to be done in stages. The machines would read the initial data from punched cards, perform the calculations and punch results onto a new set of cards. Then the equipment would be reset to carry out the mathematics of the next stage, using the cards with the intermediate results as input. Complicated jobs could require a lot of effort in setting up the machines and keeping the intermediate cards in order.

Even before the war, some scientists had discerned a need to reduce the amount of human intervention in the computing process. One was Howard Aiken. In 1937, while doing graduate work in physics at Harvard, Aiken had outlined his ideas of the features required for a scientific computer: It should be fully automatic; it should be capable of handling positive and negative numbers and carrying out calculations in a sequence natural to mathematicians; and it should be able to utilize a variety of mathematical functions, such as the sines and cosines of trigonometry. "Because of the greater complexity of scientific problems as compared to accounting problems," Aiken emphasized, "the number of arithmetical elements would have to be greatly increased." By "arithmetical elements," he meant those parts of the machine that actually perform the calculations, as opposed to moving data or printing it, for example.

All of these features, Aiken believed, could be incorporated into existing IBM machines. His proposal came to the attention of T.H. Brown, a Harvard Business School professor who was a member of the Board of Managers for Columbia's Computing Bureau. Brown arranged for Aiken to visit Wallace Eckert and his associates, and this in turn led to an agreement between Aiken and IBM to pursue his concept.

The resulting machine was the Automatic Sequence Controlled Calculator, or Mark I. It was developed by Aiken and a team of Harvard scientists working in collaboration with a group of IBM engineers under the same·Clair Lake who had modified punched-card machines for Eckert. Unlike Eckert's machines, the Mark I read data from continuous punched-paper tapes. It also demanded less of its human operators, since intermediate results could be held inside the computer until needed. In other respects, though, the Mark I was like a whole series of punched-card machines linked into one unit. Completed in 1944, it was more than 50 feet long and eight feet high, with 750,000 components connected by 500 miles of wiring. Visitors likened the sound of its 3,000 switches opening and closing to the clatter of myriad knitting needles.

The Mark I, receiving instructions and data punched out on four long paper tapes, could add three eight-digit numbers per second, exceeding the capacity of the old punched-card tabulator in Columbia's Astronomical Computing Bureau. But its attraction for scientists lay in its ability to compute complicated division and trigonometric problems in less than a minute. Indeed, the Mark I's staff nicknamed it Bessie because of its ability to compute Bessel functions, which are solutions to certain kinds of differential equations. The constraints of war, however, meant that it performed no pure scientific work during the early part of its 16-year career. Shortly after it was built, it was leased to the navy, which used it to solve ballistics problems.

ELECTRONIC SOLUTIONS

The speed and versatility of the Mark I were soon challenged by the world's first electronic digital computer, the Electronic Numerical Integrator and Computer (ENIAC), built at the University of Pennsylvania's Moore School of Electrical Engineering. The designers of ENIAC, John Mauchly and J. Presper Eckert (no relation to Wallace Eckert), did away with the relays and mechanical counters that were the heart of punched-card calculating machines. Instead, they used more than 18,000 vacuum tubes. Working at electronic speeds, ENIAC could perform additions a thousand times faster than the Mark I and multiplications 500 times faster. In development for three years, ENIAC went into operation in 1945, too late to assist the war effort; but it remained in service for many years at the U.S. Army's Aberdeen Proving Ground in Maryland, where it compiled ballistics tables with great speed. The hundreds of multiplications and additions required to work out a single trajectory required only 20 seconds to compute—10 seconds less than a shell would take to reach its target.

ENIAC's technical superiority offended IBM's Thomas Watson, who was determined to keep his company in the forefront of scientific calculating. Watson was also bitterly resentful of what he believed was failure on Howard Aiken's part to acknowledge IBM's role in the creation of the Mark I. Late in 1944, he gave his engineers a clear statement of his expectations: They should develop a "super calculator" that would be in a class with ENIAC; the new machine should far surpass the Mark I, consigning it and its offspring to technological oblivion. To help with the effort, he invited Wallace Eckert to join IBM as the first director of the company's new Pure Science Department. Eckert was also

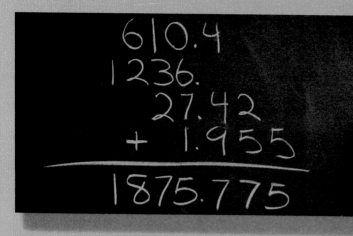

Hand addition yields precise answers because there is no limit to number length. Here, the total runs to seven digits, reflecting all the places—from thousands to thousandths—spanned by the numbers being added.

Stratagems for Accuracy

In the world of science, whether mapping the surface of the sea *(pages 100-101)* or charting the orbits of the planets, computers are virtuoso number-crunchers. Yet, for all their mathematical prowess, they perform less than perfectly with numbers having extremely long strings of digits, common in scientific enterprises.

Any figure a computer manipulates must be able to fit into the machine's word size—the number of bits, or binary digits, in a single memory location. The average personal computer has a word length of 16 bits, while the most powerful supercomputers have word lengths of up to 64 bits. Yet, numbers in science often have so many digits that some must be sacrificed. Even though the digits are struck from the right end

Truncation. Adding numbers a pair at a time in no particular order, a computer programmed to truncate drops rightmost digits as necessary to limit an answer to four places. The smallest number, 1.955, loses nearly half its value. Errors add up with each step, changing the total by almost 2.

Rounding. The computer achieves a more accurate result by rounding, which changes the smallest number by only .045—from 1.955 to 2. By rounding this number up, the computer balances some of the error introduced in the first two additions, where the numbers round down.

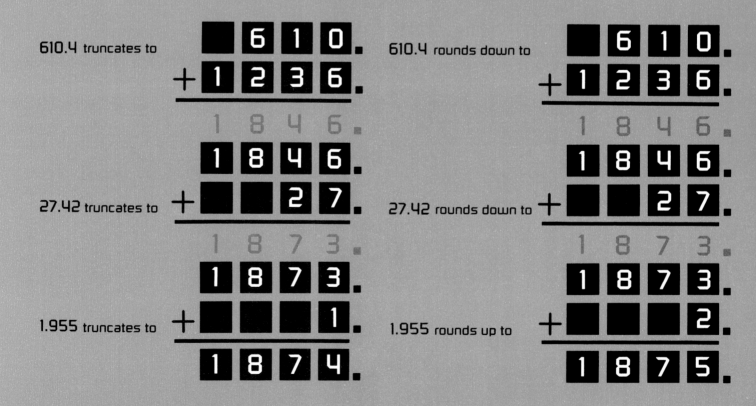

610.4 truncates to

27.42 truncates to

1.955 truncates to

610.4 rounds down to

27.42 rounds down to

1.955 rounds up to

of a number, where they are least significant, the computer thereafter produces inaccurate results.

Computers shorten numbers either by truncation or by rounding. Truncation chops off digits without regard for their value—usually the fastest and easiest method but also the most inaccurate. In rounding, the computer examines digits before discarding them. If the leftmost digit of those to be shed equals or exceeds 5, the rightmost digit that will remain after rounding is increased by 1. Otherwise, the rightmost digit is not changed. The rounding process may slow calculations, but the process almost always yields more accurate results than truncating.

Whether a computer calculates by truncating or rounding,

small errors can accumulate over a long series of calculations. Furthermore, as shown on the blackboard at left, an answer can grow longer than its components and require further shortening. Computer designers have developed stratagems to minimize these effects. One is to allocate two words per number, an approach known as double precision because it provides memory space for twice as many digits. Other methods, such as the one shown on this page, improve accuracy by reorganizing the work.

All four examples below assume an imaginary computer capable of handling numbers no more than four digits. For clarity, decimal numbers have been used rather than the binary zeros and ones of a real computer.

Ordered truncation. Adding the numbers in numerical order from smallest to largest minimizes truncating errors. In the first two calculations, the computer can include digits to the right of the decimal point, thereby retaining some of their value in the answer.

Ordered rounding. Rearrangement before rounding produces the most accurate answer—only .225 greater than the total on the blackboard. Once again, the computer retains more of the smaller numbers' digits by adding them first. Rounding then keeps each subtotal closer to the true value.

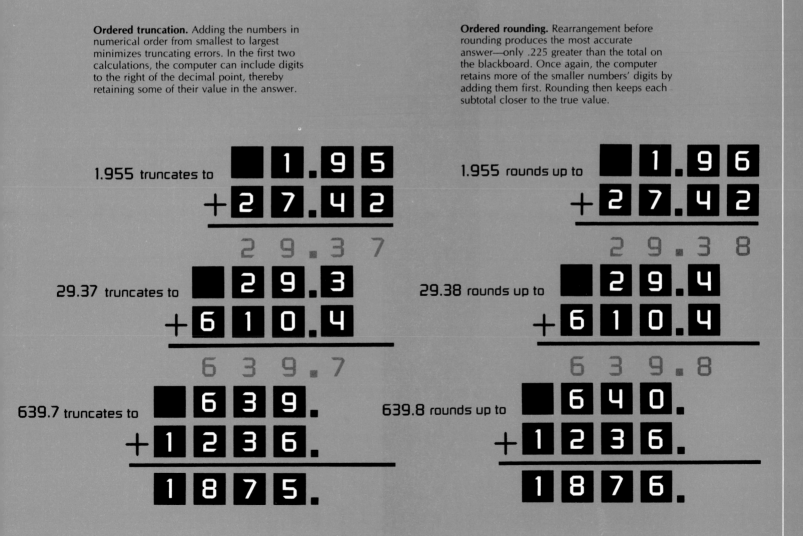

1.955 truncates to ■ 1.95
+ 27.42
2 9 . 3 7

29.37 truncates to ■ 29.3
+ 610.4
6 3 9 . 7

639.7 truncates to ■ 639.
+ 1236.
1875.

1.955 rounds up to ■ 1.96
+ 27.42
2 9 . 3 8

29.38 rounds up to ■ 29.4
+ 610.4
6 3 9 . 8

639.8 rounds up to ■ 640.
+ 1236.
1876.

given the role of organizing yet another Columbia-affiliated monument to the IBM chief's philanthropy: the Watson Scientific Computing Laboratory. Unlike the Astronomical Computing Bureau, the Scientific Computing Laboratory was intended for use by scientists in any field; the facilities were made available, free of charge, to people whose scientific problems were of particular interest. This interest, Eckert made clear, "may be manifested in the computational aspects of the problem or in results which will be of importance to science."

From the start, Eckert was closely involved with the engineers working on Watson's super calculator. Although he was primarily a user of calculating equipment rather than a designer, he had always relished the challenge of adapting standard equipment to achieve unprecedented computing capabilities. His experience made him the ideal choice to lay down the specifications for a machine that would meet the needs of general scientific users. By March 1946, these specifications had been agreed upon. The new machine, to be called the Selective Sequence Electronic Calculator (SSEC), would be a large-scale, general-purpose calculator combining ease of use with electronic speed in its arithmetic section. The sequence of operations would be controlled by means of instructions stored in a hierarchy of memories that included electronic, electromechanical and punched paper-tape sections. Not surprisingly, Eckert also specified a large and flexible table-checking capability: Users could store scientific tables in the machine, which would refer to them automatically during computations.

What these specifications added up to was a machine able to tackle far more complex problems than any other computer then in existence. The SSEC was not, however, meant to represent a breakthrough in computer technology. It was designed to extract the maximum performance from vacuum tubes and electromechanical devices already in use. In truth, the SSEC was a hybrid of the old electromechanical computers, typified by the Mark I, and the new generation of electronic machines exemplified by the ENIAC.

Once the specifications had been approved, Eckert exercised rather distant supervision over the team charged with development of the SSEC. The chief engineer for the computer was Frank Hamilton, who had played a major part in directing the design and construction of the Mark I. He was complemented by Robert "Rex" Seeber, a Harvard mathematician who had worked for Howard Aiken as a programmer on the Mark I. Seeber left Harvard when Aiken rejected his suggestion that a computer ought to be designed so that instructions could be stored and operated on as data, a concept that later proved essential to modern computer design.

RACE TO COMPLETION
The schedule called for the new machine to be ready in the beginning of 1947, one year after Watson tapped Hamilton for the job. By the end of the year, the team was working around the clock, struggling to meet the deadline. One impediment had been the difficulty of finding reliable power supplies, the parts that deliver carefully regulated electric current to the rest of the machine. When the engineers finally located a source for these components, the Power Equipment Company (PECo) of Detroit, they ordered all the parts then available, stressing that the project would be seriously delayed if the shipment was lost or

damaged. Despite PECo's best efforts, the deadline for completing the computer passed unmet before the company could arrange to ship the badly needed components. Final wiring and preliminary testing remained to be done, and neither task could be accomplished without the power supplies. To expedite the shipment, Sam Hanley, president of PECo, arranged with one of Detroit's best trucking firms for direct delivery to IBM's Endicott production facility. Moreover, he had the firm insure the shipment for a million dollars, demanded that they assign their most trustworthy drivers to the job, and insisted that on no account should they try getting through if the roads were hazardous. Hanley then called Endicott to tell them to expect delivery, but warned that it might be delayed several days, since heavy snow was forecast for that night on all routes east of Detroit.

"The next morning," recalled Byron Phelps, one of the Endicott team, "we found the truck waiting for us at the loading dock." The drivers had driven 500 miles through heavy snow. After using up all the cinders in a device that automatically spread them under the wheels of the truck for traction, they had continued despite slippery hills. Loading the deck behind the truck cab with sand from roadside emergency supplies, they proceeded with one man shoveling sand under the truck wheels while the other drove. "If Hanley or we had known," Phelps said, "we probably would have had a heart attack, and most certainly would have sent the police after them." As it was, the parts worked well, and PECo became for years the leading source of computer power supplies in the United States.

Meanwhile, quarters to house the SSEC had been prepared. As IBM's showpiece, the computer would be installed in a building on 57th Street in Manhattan, right next to the company's Madison Avenue headquarters. When it became clear that the new machine, a 60-foot-long monster, would leave no room in the building for its power supplies, IBM bought out a shoe store around the corner and installed the support equipment there.

Thomas Watson did not wholly approve of the accommodation. A man of strong dislikes, he took exception to the six marble pillars in the computer room on the grounds that they were not in keeping with a technological image. He ordered them removed. Everyone present nodded dutifully, but since they knew the pillars were holding the building up, the people charged with executing the order eventually decided on a compromise: The pillars were left in place; the glossy publicity photographs of the exhibition room were touched up to show that they had been removed.

By mid-1947, the SSEC was installed, its cabinets of vacuum tubes and relays neatly arranged on three sides of the air-conditioned, fireproof room. The engineering team began intensive testing and debugging, which continued to the very hour of the machine's dedication on January 27, 1948. On the morning of the great day, the chances of a successful demonstration of its powers at the ceremony seemed remote, mainly because of the likelihood of failure among the computer's 12,500 vacuum tubes. These were radio tubes, built to ordinary commercial standards and often subject to intermittent short-circuiting lasting only a millionth of a second—not noticeable in a radio, but likely to cause an error in the operation of a digital circuit. In addition, the construction and decorating work that went on around the SSEC until the last minute generated airborne debris, which caused serious malfunctions in the 21,400 relays.

Given these adversities, the suspense was almost palpable at the formal luncheon preceding the machine's inaugural run. Thomas Watson—turning a blind eye to the pillars—rose to dedicate the SSEC "to the use of science throughout the world." Then Eckert described the problem he had selected to put the SSEC through its paces—the computation of an improved lunar ephemeris. Eckert and his colleagues watched anxiously while Seeber began the program. As many of those present later recalled with wonder, the machine ran all afternoon without a hitch. Eckert, in fact, went on to compute the moon's position at half-day intervals for every day from 1952 through 1971.

In its setting of marble and stainless steel, the computer was plainly visible to passing pedestrians. For months, hundreds of them gathered at the large window to gaze at the display. Inside, reported a journalist who was allowed entry, "there is the quiet clicking of printers, the steady shuffling of punched cards, the occasional rotation of a drum with 'memory' tape, and a continual dance of little red lights as number-indicating tubes flick on and off in far less time than the twinkling of an eye. All else is hushed, and even the operators speak quietly in this streamlined sanctuary." Inspired by the machine's banks of lights and tape reels, cartoonists fixed for a generation the public's conception of what a computer should look like.

Yet despite the SSEC's futuristic image, its electromechanical components made it obsolescent at birth. It was switched off for good in the summer of 1952 and dismantled to make way in the showroom for a Model 701. The 701 was IBM's first all-electronic computer; unlike the SSEC, it was built in quantity and leased to customers. But in the SSEC's short working life, this last of the mechanical monsters brought home to the scientific community the potential of computers in research. Faithful to its vow, IBM provided free use of the SSEC in solving problems of pure science. Besides being applied to astronomical projects, the computer was used to solve problems involving fluid flow, nuclear physics and optics. Eckert himself would have good cause to remember the SSEC's contribution to science when, in 1969, high-precision tables that it had produced were used to plot the course of the space vehicle that first took men to the moon.

A Game of Evolution

There is no way to experiment on a star. All are too big, too energetic and too far away for manipulation by mere humans. A direct check of a new idea about a star is thus impossible; the only way to test a supposition about a star's energy production, for example, is by calculation. The process is simple to describe: Assume that the idea is correct, create equations relating energy production to other characteristics of stars and then observe stars to see if the measured characteristics match those predicted by the new equations. The difficulty lies in performing the calculations. Doing the mathematics necessary to simulate the development of a star from birth to death would take an astrophysicist 3,000 years—without a computer. With an ordinary laboratory computer, the task can be done in hours.

To accomplish such a feat, the computer is invested with an experimental system, a model mimicking a natural system that is too difficult to study in the real world. This approach has already transformed the way scientists and engineers test the informed guesses they call hypotheses. Chemists view diagrams of hypothetical molecules on monitor screens, then apply computer programs that predict how the molecules will interact. Ecologists forecast the effects that pollutants will have on the atmosphere in the decades ahead.

Each experiment is much like a computerized game in which the scientist defines the rules as well as the nature of the players. The games master first programs into the computer the various components of the system and specifies mathematically the ways they interact. Because natural systems are so complex, the models are simplified to include as rules of the game only those aspects of the natural system that seem critical to the hypothesis.

Next, the scientist sets the game in motion. In the model described on the following pages, which tests a hypothesis about the course of evolution, the computer grows an eon's worth of forests composed of many trees with thousands of limbs to see how trees' light-gathering ability and the strength of their branches affected the evolution of tree shapes.

Finally, the scientist compares the model's results with observations of the real world. If they differ, either the model or the hypothesis is flawed. If they are similar, the hypothesis is supported, but not proved. Because a model is a simplification of reality, it cannot conclusively prove anything.

Making the Rules

No computer is needed to trace the earliest stages of evolution in the most distant ancestors of modern trees and bushes. Fossils show that this evolutionary line started out, 450 million years ago, as straggly growths with few branches and no leaves. Food was produced in stems and branches, which were sensitive to light. Over the following 130 million years, plants evolved into a variety of forms: some tall with central trunks, others bushy with horizontal fans of branches. Although the fossils demonstrate that these changes in structure took place, no evidence tells why.

Simple logic suggests an answer. Presumably, the plants assumed shapes that exposed their food-producing branches to greater amounts of sunlight. But the progress would have been subject to limits. Even as the plants responded to the sun by sprouting more branches at angles that caught more light, branching would have been restricted by mechanical stress: Certain branching patterns would make a plant fall over or cause its stems to snap.

This hypothesis is one that Karl J. Niklas and his colleagues at Cornell University set out to test with computer modeling. Mathematical formulas to calculate and compare the opposing forces became the rules of the game in Niklas' program, which also supplied the players—plants that changed shape in specified ways (right). The winner in each round of the game represented an evolutionary step, the emergence of one species from another.

Ancient plants, shown in the landscape at left as they appeared toward the middle of the period covered by the Niklas experiment, had to be simplified for his model. He reduced them to stick figures having only the three physical characteristics described below.

Which stems branch? One feature of a simulated tree species is its probability of branching, which determines whether a stem grows two daughters or a single extension each time that it buds (*purple branches, left*).

Vertical or horizontal? The model's second characteristic is the branching angle between two daughter branches (*orange*) emerging from the same parent stem (*green*). With a small angle, new stems increase plant height and minimize mechanical stress. Plants with large angles expose more branches to sunlight but also increase stress.

Compact or spread out? A pair of new stems can turn with respect to the parent, but only if the parent, too, was part of a pair. The angle of rotation, if minimized, makes the simulated plant fanlike; if maximized, globular. The purple fork, for example, is rotated 50 degrees from the orange fork.

The three characteristics, which give each computer-generated plant a slightly different pattern of branches, can be marked off on three mutually perpendicular axes of a three-dimensional graph (*below*), creating a cubical space. Within this cube, each point represents one species of plant possessing a unique combination of characteristics.

Creating
the Players

Once the rules are set, the hypothesis-testing game can begin. It proceeds in two alternating stages. In the first, illustrated on this and the facing page, the computer model grows examples of a single species of tree and deduces its fitness for survival. In the second stage *(pages 26-27)*, the model matches the species against others similar to it that the computer has grown in the same manner.

The starting point for the game comes from fossils, which can be measured to give the particular branching angle, rotation angle and branching probability characterizing a plant that actually existed long ago. The computer generates 10 of that species to the forms that they would reach after 10 branching cycles. All these simulated plants have identical-branching and rotation angles, but, because the branching probability is less than 100 percent *(right)*, they do not all branch at the same points. Thus, each of the 10 examples differs slightly in form from the others.

Next, the computer calculates the light-gathering ability of each computer-generated plant and averages the figures. Similar computations yield an average for mechanical stresses. Finally, the first average is divided by the second to get a ratio of fitness. The greater the light-gathering ability of a species compared with the stresses on it—that is, the greater its food production compared with its chances of breaking under its own weight—the more likely the species is to survive and contribute to the next stage in computerized evolution.

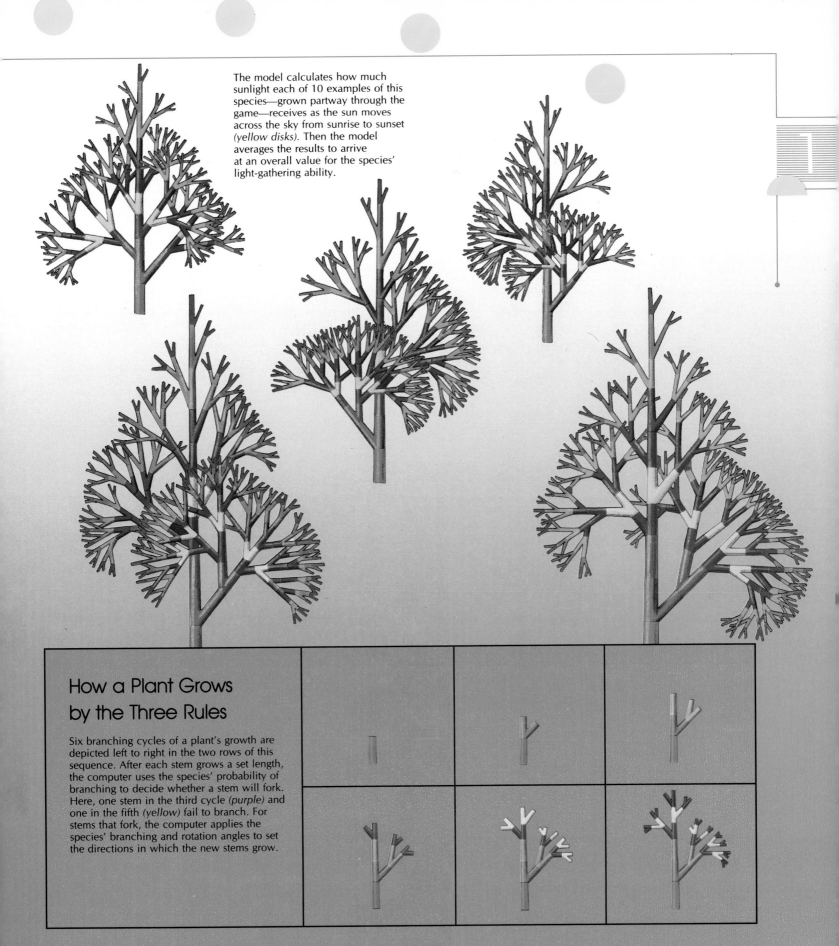

The model calculates how much sunlight each of 10 examples of this species—grown partway through the game—receives as the sun moves across the sky from sunrise to sunset *(yellow disks)*. Then the model averages the results to arrive at an overall value for the species' light-gathering ability.

How a Plant Grows by the Three Rules

Six branching cycles of a plant's growth are depicted left to right in the two rows of this sequence. After each stem grows a set length, the computer uses the species' probability of branching to decide whether a stem will fork. Here, one stem in the third cycle *(purple)* and one in the fifth *(yellow)* fail to branch. For stems that fork, the computer applies the species' branching and rotation angles to set the directions in which the new stems grow.

Playing the Game
to Find the Fittest

Two fundamental processes drive evolution. First, changes in an organism's hereditary material (its DNA) alter the characteristics of succeeding generations. Second, the best alterations, or mutations, are perpetuated through natural selection, a culling process survived only by mutations that help the organism adapt to its environment.

In this computer-modeled experiment, the two evolutionary processes are imitated in a series of contests—rounds of a game, in effect—that test species against one another. The players in each round can be visualized as 27 squares drawn in layers (left). At the center of the middle layer is the starting

point for the arrangement—either the fossil-based plant that begins the game or the winner of the previous round. To simulate mutation, the computer generates 26 closely related species (the other squares) by changing one or more of the center species' three characteristics—its branching angle, rotation angle and branching probability. For each species, the ratio of light-gathering ability to mechanical stress is determined in the manner described on the preceding pages. The species with the highest ratio—the fittest—is judged the survivor (brightest green) and becomes the point of departure for the next round of mutation and selection.

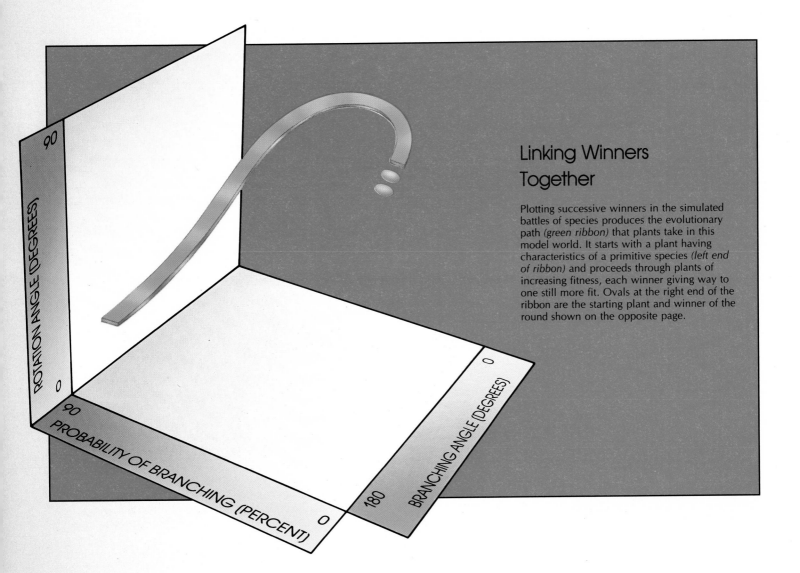

Linking Winners Together

Plotting successive winners in the simulated battles of species produces the evolutionary path (green ribbon) that plants take in this model world. It starts with a plant having characteristics of a primitive species (left end of ribbon) and proceeds through plants of increasing fitness, each winner giving way to one still more fit. Ovals at the right end of the ribbon are the starting plant and winner of the round shown on the opposite page.

ROTATION ANGLE (DEGREES)

90

0

PROBABILITY OF BRANCHING (PERCENT)

90

0

BRANCHING ANGLE (DEGREES)

0

180

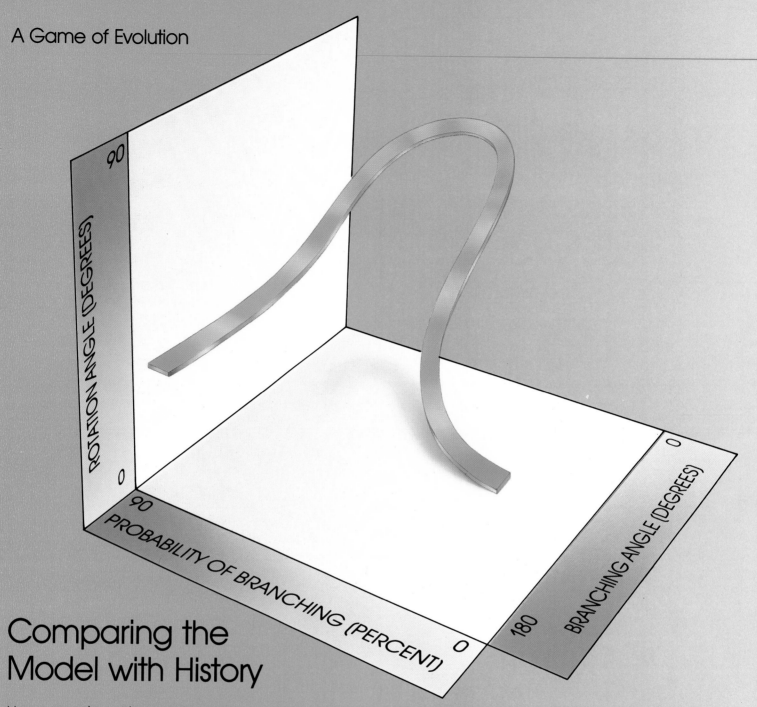

ROTATION ANGLE (DEGREES)

90

0

PROBABILITY OF BRANCHING (PERCENT)

90

0

BRANCHING ANGLE (DEGREES)

0

180

Comparing the Model with History

Now comes the acid test—comparing the model's output with the fossil record to see if there is any resemblance between the two. In this case, the predictions are approximately borne out. The path generated by the computer, represented as a green ribbon in the cubical space above, traces the evolution of simulated plants having structures that resemble actual fossils. Computer-generated plants, like real ones, tend to develop a central stem with lateral branches. That the computer images look somewhat like fossils, however, does not prove the hypothesis. Different theories—and other models—could produce equally convincing simulations.

Very often, a model produces results that are completely at odds with observations of the real world. When faced with such discrepancies. a scientist tinkers with varioius details of the model. Perhaps the methods for calculating light-gathering ability were wrong, or some of the simplifying assumptions were invalid. For example, this model assumed that plants cast no shadows on one another, but mutual shading may in fact have been an important factor in evolution. Introducing other physical characteristics, such as the bending of branches, may produce a better match with reality, but at the expense of much longer computer runs.

If changes in the model's details do not bring its predictions closer to reality, the hypothesis itself could be faulty. Though initially disappointing, such a result may really be welcome. Eliminating one idea simply narrows the search for truth.

450 million years ago: Rhyniophytes

The oldest fossils believed to be precursors to the ancestors of trees and bushes are those of rhyniophytes *(far right)*; these plants were sparsely branched, grew about two feet tall and collected light energy through green stems. Their characteristics provided the initial state for the model, which generated a computer image that, except for the tall starting stem, looks much like the real plant.

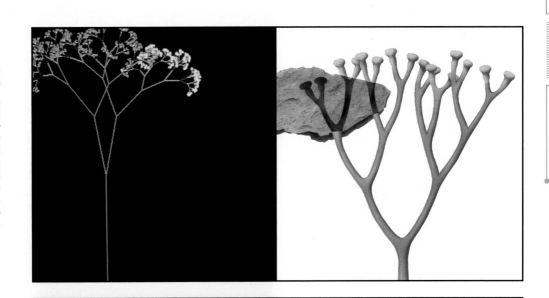

380 million years ago: Trimerophytes

The next major group in the evolution of trees and bushes were the trimerophytes *(far right)*. The model simulated, partway through its run, a plant resembling trimerophytes in that the computer version had more branches than predecessor plants and many of the branches extended sideways from a readily discernible stem. Trimerophytes gave rise to a variety of primitive plants before dying out, losers in the game of evolution.

320 million years ago: Progymnosperms

Among the earliest leaf-bearing plants were the progymnosperms *(far right)*. A computer simulation, produced near the end of the model's run, bears a strong resemblance to this ancient plant, which some scientists believe was a step in the evolution of conifers. The simulated plant, like modern pines and firs, has a definite vertical trunk and lateral branches.

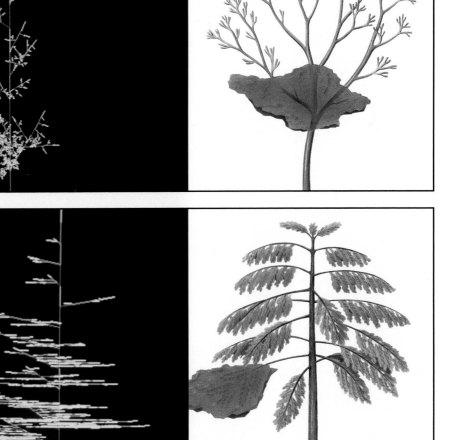

Software
for Science

Nuclear fission, the process at the heart of the atomic bomb, is easy to understand in principle: Energy is released when protons and neutrons, the particles that form the nucleus of an atom, are split apart. In a radioactive substance such as uranium, a neutron from a decaying nucleus smashes into the nucleus of another atom; among the resulting fragments are more neutrons, which go on to break up additional nuclei. The exponentially increasing cascade of collisions is called a chain reaction.

The process of starting and maintaining a chain reaction is one that demands a fairly detailed understanding of the behavior of neutrons. This is something not easily arrived at: The activity of neutrons in a chain reaction is much too fast and too minuscule in scale for direct observation. Therefore, as the study of nuclear reactions for both military and commercial uses intensified in the latter part of the 1940s, scientists tried to simulate the process, doing step-by-step calculations to work out how one generation of collisions would lead to the next. The computational challenge was huge because of the numbers involved: A single triggering neutron produces more than a billion offspring in just 30 generations of collisions.

Nuclear scientists, in order to speed their calculations, were hoping to employ the emerging technology of electronic computers; the new machines, however, were proving to be something less than a panacea. They were difficult to use, so it was necessary that specialists in any discipline learn the fundamentals of computer science before the equipment could be put to work. Furthermore, the machines often lacked the power to handle the largest scientific problems in reasonable spans of time.

Advances in computer hardware—that is, in the machine itself—would play an important role in broadening the usefulness of the new technology. But in nuclear physics and in other scientific fields, some of the most important boosts to the utility of computers came from innovations in software—the programs, or lists of instructions, that tell the computer what to do and when to do it.

As the computer age gained momentum, the machines were harnessed to scientific work by a wealth of ingenious software. Some of it, like the so-called Monte Carlo method of computer modeling, introduced entirely new ways for scientists to explore the natural world. Some consisted of easy-to-use programming languages that made it possible for scientists to produce their own specialized software without having to first acquire a detailed knowledge of the computer. Other software armed scientists with a complete arsenal of mathematical skills, incorporating the knowledge of many experts. And thousands of programs took over some of the mundane tasks of science, such as monitoring experiments and sorting data.

One of the first big breakthroughs—and one particularly important for scientists—was the Monte Carlo method, which uses approximations based on random numbers to produce much more accurate solutions for a whole class of problems, including many in nuclear physics. The story of its discovery and dissemination is a case study of how a few remarkable individuals have enlarged the scope of scientific computing.

The Monte Carlo method was conceived by Polish-born Stanislaw Ulam, one of a generation of talented mathematicians who came of age in Eastern Europe in the years between the two world wars. As an 11-year-old boy in the 1920s, Ulam had attended—and, to the amazement of his elders, understood—lectures on Albert Einstein's newly proposed general theory of relativity. In the mid-1930s, Ulam, who by then had a Ph.D. in mathematics, began a correspondence with John von Neumann, a brilliant Hungarian mathematician and logician who had won a position at Princeton's Institute for Advanced Study. Impressed by Ulam's published work, von Neumann invited him to come to the institute for a few months. Ulam arrived in late 1935 and was swept up in the intellectual ferment. At the time, Princeton was a way station for European scientists fleeing the threat of Nazi persecution. Along with von Neumann, Einstein was there; so was German-born Hermann Weyl, who had done much to explain the mathematical framework of Einstein's theories; so was the great Austrian mathematician Kurt Gödel. Ulam met many of these luminaries at parties that were given two or three times a week by the convivial von Neumann. As the young Pole later recalled, the gatherings were "not completely carefree; the shadow of coming world events pervaded the social atmosphere."

Ulam remained in the United States, spending three years at Harvard before he moved on to the University of Wisconsin in the spring of 1940. Although he made a return trip to Poland every summer between 1936 and 1939, the outbreak of war in Europe in September of 1939 cut him off from his family and friends. Distraught at the toll that the war was taking on his homeland, he looked for a way in which he could fight back. Just as soon as he received his U.S. citizenship papers in 1941, he tried to enlist in the Army Air Corps, but he was rejected because of poor eyesight.

His intellectual skills were unimpeachable, however. He had stayed in touch with von Neumann while at Harvard—they even traveled together during those summers in Europe—and had continued to exchange letters from Wisconsin. In 1943, von Neumann, who was by this time deeply involved in the Manhattan Project, suggested that Ulam be recruited for the bomb-building effort. Ulam accepted, obtained a leave of absence from the University of Wisconsin and boarded a train for Los Alamos, New Mexico. Once he arrived, he was put to work with physicist Edward Teller, helping develop the mathematics associated with a "super bomb," as the proposed hydrogen bomb was then called. It would work by the process of fusion, using intense heat and pressure to force the atoms of a heavy isotope of hydrogen to fuse together into helium atoms and release energy in the process.

TO LOS ALAMOS

At Los Alamos, Ulam for the first time put his theoretical acumen to work in the field of applied physics. One of his specialties, the mathematics of branching processes, was critical to understanding the behavior of neutrons in collisions with atomic nuclei. The neutron activity—just as important in the fusion reaction as in fission—could be represented in the form of a rapidly multiplying series of branches, like a tree. A collision was thought of as a branching point. At each point, a neutron might be absorbed, or continue on its path, or cause the emergence of two, three or four new neutrons, all headed for collisions of their own. None of these possible outcomes of a collision could be predicted absolutely; through repeated experiments, however, the probability of each result had been determined. The problem for physicists who were trying to understand how a fusion reaction might work was to follow the future course of the initial neutron and its progeny through the chain of possibilities that would arise from many generations of collisions. Ulam helped to chart the way in this effort. As for the actual number-crunching that was required to trace the branching chains, much of it was done with the IBM calculating machines that had been ordered for atomic bomb work.

The cultural ambiance of the Manhattan Project could be as rarefied as the air of the mountains of Los Alamos. In his native city of Lvov Ulam had delighted in communing with other mathematicians, playing chess in cafés and discussing abstruse problems. Now he was working and relaxing with many of the leading scientific thinkers of the day. A lunchtime conversation might range from the intricacies of quantum physics to speculation on the effect that nuclear experiments would have on the technology of the future. Ulam, who once estimated that he normally spent "two to three hours a day thinking and two to three hours reading or conversing about mathematics," was in his element. The natural setting of the facility was equally congenial. To keep it from looking like a military base, the project's director, Robert Oppenheimer, had insisted on preserving trees and laying out roads that curved; laboratories and houses nestled among pine trees 7,000 feet above sea level. Ulam and his wife, Françoise, were assigned to a small cottage by a pond.

BACK TO TEACHING

The end of World War II in 1945 brought a halt to this intellectual idyll. Los Alamos went onto a peacetime footing, and Ulam found himself displaced once again. War-ravaged Europe held no appeal; none of his family in Poland, and few of his friends, had survived the German occupation. Looking for a teaching job with better prospects than his old position at Wisconsin, he landed at the University of Southern California in Los Angeles. It was there, during the winter of 1945-1946, that he was struck by a near-fatal attack of viral encephalitis, which he later called "one of the most shattering experiences of my life." One by-product of the episode, however, would have profound consequences for the nascent field of scientific computing.

Emergency surgery relieved pressure on Ulam's brain, which had caused violent headaches and a loss of the ability to use words. Although these symptoms disappeared after he had the surgery, Ulam and his doctors were concerned that he might have suffered brain damage and would no longer be capable of complex mathematical reasoning. Their fears, however, were soon put to rest. As he played solitaire to while away the hours of his convalescence, Ulam got the first inklings of the Monte Carlo method.

Ulam found himself pondering the mathematical probability of winning. He realized that the most practical way to get a good idea of the odds was simply to play the game many times, noting the proportion of successful conclusions to failures. Playing more and more games would give him an increasingly accurate estimate of the odds. Even though this method could never yield absolutely precise results, it would be much easier than trying to calculate the probable occurrence of each hand mathematically. Every time a card is laid down, there are many possibilities for the next card, and for each of those potential followers, another multitude of potential successors. In fact, because a 52-card deck can be arranged in more ways than there are subatomic particles in a galaxy, calculating the outcome of every game is an impossibility.

In solitaire, Ulam saw a branching system that was similar to the thermonuclear processes he had studied at Los Alamos. At every branch—whether it was the turning over of a new card or the collision of particles—the outcome is random, in the sense that it cannot be predicted on the basis of the known facts. Each outcome, however, has a known probability of occurring. Ulam quickly realized that the method he used to find the odds in solitaire—that is to say, playing a lot of games—could also be employed to arrive at a statistical picture of the overall behavior of neutrons in collisions. In this instance, he would have to simulate many generations of collisions. At each branching point, the actions of the simulated particles would follow the same patterns as those observed in nature. Ulam realized that after many repetitions of the process, he would be able to take a look at the cumulative outcome of the simulations and then arrive at conclusions about the probable behavior of the system as a whole.

Ulam soon got a chance to apply his insight. Los Alamos was being reorganized for postwar work, and he was invited to return to the "super bomb" project. In New Mexico, he was reunited with his friend von Neumann, based again at Princeton but still a frequent visitor to the facility. During a 30-mile drive from Los Alamos to the nearest train station, Ulam proposed applying his probabilistic solution to nuclear studies. At first skeptical of the usefulness of the technique of approximation, von Neumann soon saw its potential. Both men knew from their wartime experience that the new computing machines were well suited to the volume of calculation required by the statistical approach. They also realized that questions similar to the neutron collision problem abounded in fields such as aerodynamics and meteorology.

Using the Monte Carlo method on a computer requires a program, called a model, that recreates a small part of the real world within the machine. In this

Feigning Unpredictability

Many natural phenomena—the weather or the decay of unstable atoms, for example—are inherently unpredictable. To simulate such behavior with a computer, scientists must inject a degree of unpredictability into their models by including randomly selected numbers that, like a deck of well-shuffled cards, follow no detectable pattern.

Unfortunately, haphazardness of the kind necessary to create such numbers is alien to computers, which by design never deviate from a program's strict order of steps. So scientists have settled for something called pseudorandom numbers—long sequences of values, numbering in the millions, that have all the important characteristics of truly random numbers.

There is an ingeniously simple algorithm that turns a computer into an effortless producer of strings of pseudorandom numbers. The formula, illustrated here, is as follows: Multiply an initial value, or seed, by one number, add another, divide by a third, then use the remainder both as the first value

of the random series and as the seed for the next value.

The third number in the formula determines the maximum length of the sequence—16 values for the simplified example here. The other two values must be chosen with care or the algorithm will short-circuit and begin repeating numbers. Mathematical tests reveal which values avoid this trap. The second number must not divide evenly into the third and vice versa; nor may both be divisible by the same number. Subtracting 1 from the first value must yield a result that does divide evenly into the third value.

Even with appropriate values, the computer-generated sequence eventually repeats itself, forming a necklace of numbers (below). Because the numbers exhibit no pattern of repetition within the sequence, however, they are satisfactory substitutes for true random numbers. Moreover, their cyclical nature can be a boon: By using the same random numbers in many runs of a single simulation, scientists can correct flaws in a model that they might otherwise be unable to explain.

A computer algorithm designed to mix up the numbers from 0 through 15 uses a simple arithmetic formula (above, left) to create a sequence, or necklace, of numbers in an apparently haphazard order (above). The process begins with the arbitrary selection of one number called the seed, a role played here by 4. The seed is fed into the generator, which multiplies it by 5, adds 7 to the result and divides the total, 27, by 16. The answer, 1, is discarded, and the remainder, 11, becomes both the first

bead in the necklace and a new seed, which loops back into the generator. The second time through, the generator again throws away the answer, keeping the remainder of 14 as the second necklace bead and using it as another new seed. The generator continues processing seeds and churning out beads—the next one is 13—until it has run through all 16 numbers. The sequence is complete when 4 reappears as the last bead in the necklace and the seed that begins the cycle anew.

electronic environment, events occur with the same statistical frequency as observed in nature. At each branching point in the simulated process, the computer consults a set of options and chooses what will happen next. The choice, which is governed by the output of a random-number generator *(pages 36-37)* is based on previously determined probabilities. For example, a simple model might be designed with three possible courses at every single branching point: Option A, with a 60 percent probability of being chosen; Option B, with a 30 percent chance; and Option C, with a 10 percent chance. In this scenario, if the random-number generator provides numbers from 1 to 1,000 (a real model would use far more), each time a number from 1 to 600 appears, the model would select Option A and proceed to the next branching point. A number from 601 to 900 would cause the model to choose Option B. And a number from 901 to 1,000 would make Option C the choice. In effect, the computer is rolling a set of trick dice.

The simulated system combines numerous probabilistic branches—thousands of them in the case of the neutron collision problem. Each time the computer model is run, the combination of all the random branches produces a result that is unique . But if the model is run enough times, a statistically average result can be determined. The result is never an exact answer. Instead, it is, as Ulam expressed it, an indication that "the answer is so and so, within such and such an error, with such and such probability."

GETTING THE WORD OUT
Helpful in developing the technique, von Neumann was invaluable in spreading it. A singular scientific generalist, he was capable of conversing at the highest levels in a broad range of scientific fields. By 1946, he was already deeply involved in computer development. One of his jobs at Los Alamos had been working with theoreticians to adapt their problems—such as the hydrodynamics inside the imploding core of the bomb—to the capabilities of the calculating equipment that was available at the time. During World War II, he had also consulted regularly on the EDVAC computer project at the University

of Pennsylvania's Moore School of Electrical Engineering. At the end of 1945, he began work on a project to build a computer at Princeton under the auspices of the Institute for Advanced Studies, which was fast becoming an important center for the study of computing. Von Neumann turned the Monte Carlo idea over to mathematicians at the institute, who continued to work on refining it. And in his travels around the country, he acted as a tireless missionary for the new technique. Ulam also traveled in behalf of the Monte Carlo method; he referred to his discussions as "propaganda talks."

By 1949, the method had found many applications, although a certain amount of improvisation was clearly in evidence. At a Monte Carlo symposium held that year in Los Angeles, a group of mathematicians, statisticians and physicists discussed the ways in which they were generating the random numbers required by the technique: The equipment they were using ranged from the ENIAC all the way down to a spinning cylinder that had been fabricated from a Quaker Oats container. IBM punched-card calculators and tabulators were in common use among the Monte Carlo users at the symposium, and one of the participants described a project that may have been the largest ever conducted with this kind of electromechanical equipment. It was a neutron attenuation study, a simulation that was designed to examine the rate at which neutrons are scattered or absorbed as they pass through matter. During the course of the project, an IBM card-programmed calculator developed 10,000 particle life histories—for which some 2.5 million punched cards had to pass through the calculator, and many more cards than that had gone through the sorting and tabulating equipment.

But technical progress was leaving punched-card calculators behind. The growing popularity of the Monte Carlo method was closely linked with the spread of electronic computers beyond government-funded nuclear research centers. By the early part of the 1950s, scientists were using Monte Carlo simulations to explore phenomena such as the turbulent airflow around high-speed jet planes or the birth and development of storms over the ocean. The decades that followed saw simulations of every size and shape. Supercomputers modeled the big bang that spawned the universe; inexpensive desktop machines simulated the ecology of African grasslands. The common thread in all of these simulations was the method that had grown out of Stan Ulam's game of solitaire.

COMPUTERS SPREAD OUT

In 1949, IBM, responding to the growing interest in computers among scientists, established an applied sciences department. It was headed by Cuthbert C. Hurd, a mathematician who had directed technical research at a plant in Oak Ridge, Tennessee, where uranium was enriched for use in atomic bombs. At first, the department helped IBM field representatives show engineers, scientists and other current or potential customers how to utilize the company's card-programmed calculators, smaller cousins to the SSEC. But Hurd's department was also given the mandate of appraising the need for high-speed computing; within only a few years, it became a division and was producing the first electronic computers that IBM brought to market.

Working closely with their scientific customers, IBM representatives soon learned that the task of programming—listing for the computer the operations it must perform to do a particular job—was a major impediment to use of the machines. At the time, programming was usually done by writing machine code, binary instructions that govern each minuscule step of the electronic activity in a computer. It was a tedious and error-ridden process that required detailed understanding of how the various electronic elements worked together to perform even the simplest operation, such as the addition of two integers. Some computers offered a slightly more convenient alternative, called assembly language. This allowed the programmer to substitute less forgettable abbreviations and word fragments for the binary digits of machine code; the computer itself would translate the completed program into machine code. Even so, assembly language still demanded that the programmer have an intimate knowledge of the computer, and writing even relatively simple programs remained a slow business. Some programmers referred to their work as "hand-to-hand combat" with the computer.

John Backus, a veteran of the SSEC project, noted that at some of the sites where IBM's new 701 computer was installed, the combined salaries of the programming staff equaled the rental cost of the machine, on the order of $15,000 per month. He also found that as much as 40 percent of the useful computing time was expended on the process of preparing and correcting new programs, rather than on performing the intensive calculations for which the costly machines were intended. Overall, this meant that nearly three quarters of the average operating budget was consumed by programming. Backus recommended to his superiors that IBM provide its customers with a tool to ease this burden. Specifically, he suggested that for the 704, a new and more powerful machine that was soon to be introduced in the marketplace, the company develop a programming language of English-like commands. The easily understood commands, each of which would stand for a specific sequence of machine operations, would be translated into machine code by a special program called a compiler.

Late in 1953, Backus was allowed to start the compiler project, working with Harlan Herrick, another alumnus of the SSEC team. A few months later at a conference on programming, Backus and Herrick defined their goal: to make it possible for scientists and engineers to list their instructions for the computer "in a concise, fairly natural mathematical language." No longer would programmers labor over obscure references to different parts of the computer, known as memory addresses. "The programmer would like to write 'X' instead of some specific address," they said, "and if he wants to add X and Y he would like to write 'X+Y'." To do this in assembly language, by contrast, required the writing of code that would summon the values of X and Y from their locations in memory, direct the computer's arithmetic unit to add them together, and then send the result to another memory location.

Backus and his team—which eventually grew to more than a dozen, including prospective users from the Livermore National Laboratory and United Aircraft—spent three years creating a compiler called FORTRAN (for FORmula TRANslator). With its release in April 1957, the powerful new programming tool was rapidly disseminated to facilities with IBM computers. At first programmers resisted, arguing that a mere computer program like FORTRAN could not put together machine code as efficient as the results of their hand-coding. But their reluctance was usually short-lived. Bruce Rosenblatt, a programmer at Standard Oil of California, later told the story of being given a problem to solve by writing an assembly-language program, while a colleague worked on the same problem with FORTRAN. The FORTRAN programmer worked his ordinary hours and at the end of the week went home, his program written and the problem solved. Rosenblatt, working extensive overtime and through the weekend, came up with a program by the following Monday morning. "I thought my solution was better," Rosenblatt recalled, "but the handwriting was on the wall. We quickly became FORTRAN advocates."

Another early convert was the Westinghouse-Bettis Atomic Power Laboratory near Pittsburgh, where FORTRAN supplanted assembly language in simulations of the interior of a nuclear reactor. Before the introduction of FORTRAN at the laboratory, a relatively simple model had required approximately 30,000 lines of assembly code. Although far more complex simulations would be needed in order to incorporate the rapidly growing understanding of the reactor core, Bettis engineers doubted that they would be able to write and debug the enormous amount of assembly code the work would need. Their first FORTRAN program took just one afternoon to write and ran practically without a hitch; the elated engineers estimated that an assembly-language program to solve the same problem would have taken two weeks to create and an additional one or two weeks to debug.

Scientific and technical users found FORTRAN easy to learn and natural to use, and it soon became the standard programming language for scientists and engineers. A year after FORTRAN was released, a survey of IBM 704 installations showed that more than half were already employing the compiler for a majority of their problems. And other manufacturers were quick to jump on the bandwagon, adapting the compiler to be used on their own machines. By 1961, distinct versions had been prepared for eight computers built by four different companies; a FORTRAN compiler was usually one of the first pieces of software that would be written for any new machine. Despite the emergence of myriad other compilers in the 1960s and 1970s, FORTRAN remained the most popular with scientists and engineers, continuing to evolve as the years passed.

PROBLEMS KEEP GROWING

By the 1960s, it was commonplace to see computers at universities and in scientific laboratories. Yet computational frustrations had by no means disappeared. One particularly intractable class of problems were those requiring a procedure called a Fourier transform, used in analyzing series of data from nature. Because a Fourier transform involves the solving of complex differential equations, many questions in fields such as underwater acoustics and geophysics went unanswered for lack of computing power. However, a breakthrough (appropriately known as the fast Fourier transform) occurred in the mid-1960s—and it was not as the result of a purposeful development project, but because of a fortuitous chain of events that began with the research of John Tukey, a Princeton University mathematician.

Tukey, who joined Princeton's Department of Mathematics in 1939 at the age of 24, specialized in statistical theory. During World War II, he began what would become a long association with government agencies, working at Princeton on problems of controlling the fire of weapons in aircraft and armored vehicles. By the end of the war, he was involved in computer-related projects, and this would lead him to assist John von Neumann's team in developing a design for the circuits of the Institute for Advanced Studies computer. He also became a member of the technical staff of Bell Labs, meanwhile retaining his position at Princeton.

At Bell Labs in 1946, during a lunchtime discussion of the awkwardness of the term "binary digit" (the description for a unit of information in a computer), he casually coined a word that would bring him a measure of renown in the computing community. Joining the conversation in the middle, Tukey heard the complaint and the suggested solutions, including such candidates as "bigit" and "binit." "Well," he asked in his down-East accent, "Isn't the word obviously 'bit'?" Obviously it was. In short order, the word became the common description for the fundamental ones and zeros of binary computing.

Tukey's contribution to the development of the fast Fourier transform was less casual, but it was just as dependent on chance. A distinguished career at Princeton and Bell Labs resulted in his being appointed to the president's Science Advisory Committee in 1960. At a committee meeting shortly thereafter, Richard Garwin, a physicist who worked for IBM, noticed that Tukey was writing some Fourier transforms. At the time, Garwin's own research in low-temperature physics was hampered by the cost of computer time required for this mathematical technique. When he asked Tukey about the transforms, Garwin was astonished to learn that Tukey had developed a new computational method that was much faster than the usual approach.

The standard computing procedure, or algorithm, for solving Fourier transforms was simply an electronic version of the process that had been used in hand calculations since the invention of the Fourier transform in the early part of the 19th century. The computational steps and the mathematics were structured in such a way that they would make sense to humans. But the way that numbers are actually represented in a binary computer is quite different from the common decimal forms taught in arithmetic classes. Tukey's algorithm took full advantage of the binary logic of the digital computer, thereby sharply reducing the number of machine operations that would be required before a solution could be reached.

Tukey, focusing his energies on his own work, had given little thought to spreading the word of the new algorithm. For Garwin, however, the wide range of potential applications created a dilemma. If he followed his ordinary procedure, he would give the algorithm to a programmer, who would quickly write code that would let Garwin deal with his own special problem. But Garwin realized that this new technique for computing Fourier transforms could be used in many applications that were then frustrated by potentially huge expenditures for computer time. Accordingly, he decided to accept a delay in the solution of his problem while developing a general method that IBM could supply to its scientific customers.

Garwin turned to Herman Goldstine, director of Mathematical Services at IBM. Goldstine, in turn, gave the problem to programmer James Cooley, with instructions to produce a generally applicable package. Cooley, who was newly assigned to IBM's computing center in Yorktown Heights, New York, was doing some research of his own, and he considered that to be more important. But with a bit of prodding from Garwin, he put together a program in his spare time. He turned the results over to Garwin and, for the time being, did not think much more about the subject.

Richard Garwin, however, realized the value of the new algorithm. He organized meetings with IBM scientific salesmen to tell them how this tool could help their customers, as well as increase sales, by enabling existing computers to handle previously impracticable problems. In 1965, with interest increasing, Cooley and Tukey published a paper describing the process and acknowledging Garwin's ''essential role in communication and encouragement.''

Garwin also visited laboratories and corresponded with anyone whose publications indicated that they might benefit from the fast Fourier transform. One research center that happily reported the benefits of the new technique was the Lamont Geological Observatory of Columbia University. Two seismologists there received the fast Fourier transform program through an IBM user group; when they applied it to the analysis of earthquake data, they discovered that it worked at nearly 400 times the speed of a conventional program—and performed the task with greater accuracy.

By October of 1968, interest in the fast Fourier transform had reached the point that Garwin found himself expounding on the history of the new technique at a workshop on the subject sponsored by the Institute of Electrical and Electronics Engineers. Cooley, by this point famous for his part in developing the algorithm, was the keynote speaker, and the participants included scientists who were using fast Fourier transforms in applications as diverse as the study of blood flow, the analysis of acoustical signals and the engineering of radar. Since that time, the spectrum of uses for fast Fourier transforms has expanded a good deal further—to problems such as exploring the components of musical tones, studying ocean waves and investigating the structure of the molecules of life *(pages 82-91)*.

HELP FOR THEORETICIANS

Although the work of Tukey and Cooley hitched the power of computers to one important mathematical technique, the partnership between computing and mathematics was far from fully formed in the 1960s. Little of the number-crunching power of computers was available to the theoreticians who were conducting their work in algebra, the abstract language of mathematics. FORTRAN employed common algebraic symbols, but it did not enable a computer user to solve algebraic equations. While the expression $X = Y + Z$ has meaning in FORTRAN, its only possible "solution" requires that real numerical values be assigned to Y and to Z; then the computer can calculate a value for the variable X. Yet even a beginning algebra student can manipulate the same expression into the form $Y = X - Z$.

Scientists use algebra not only as a tool for finding specific values but also for thinking about mathematical abstractions. A case in point is an algebraic expression of the theory of special relativity: $E = mc^2$. Knowing the numerical value of E is usually less important than understanding the implications of the expression as a whole. Many algebraic expressions are far more complex than $E=mc^2$. They may incorporate thousands of terms and pose an Everest-like challenge to a paper-and-pencil approach. Such expressions are common for scientists who are studying such problems as the behavior of subatomic particles, for example, or the interaction of stars and galaxies.

In the late 1950s, computer scientists began trying to develop systems that could work with algebraic expressions. Rather than transforming numerical data into numerical results, computers would be required to recognize the patterns of symbols that make up equations and to manipulate them according to the rules of algebra. By the middle of the 1960s, the theory and practice of computer algebra was a lively topic, particularly at the Massachusetts Institute of Technology. It was in M.I.T.'s computing lab in 1968 that a pair of young researchers in computerized mathematics, Bill Martin and Joel Moses, got together with computer scientist Carl Engelmann, who had already produced a rudimentary algebraic manipulation system called MATHLAB. The three of them together decided to develop a much more sophisticated system, which would incorporate Martin's and Moses' ideas, the concepts embodied in MATHLAB and the best features of other systems.

Work on the program, with funding from ARPA (the Department of Defense's Advanced Research Projects Agency), began in July of 1969. The programming involved in MATHLAB was already substantial; the new system required thousands of lines of additional code, much of it written in LISP, a computer language that had been designed especially for working with symbols. By March 1971, the project was far enough advanced that seven papers were presented at a conference in Los Angeles. And the system had a name: MACSYMA. The origin of this acronym was obscure; each of the programmers later gave a different account. The first part of the name, MAC, was drawn from the name of the M.I.T. computing lab at the time; it was variously understood to stand for "multiple-access computing" (in reference to the ability of one computer to perform different jobs for several people at the same time) or "machine-aided cognition" (for the work on artificial intelligence then current in the lab). The last part of the name, SYMA, stands for "symbolic manipulator." In any case, the sense of the Latin word *maxima* (greatest) was not lost on the programmers, and Moses took pleasure in pointing out that a Hebrew word with a similar sound means "magical and wondrous."

By 1972, new programmers had joined the project, and MACSYMA was ready to be placed on ARPA's computer network, allowing other ARPA researchers to use the system by making connections over telephone lines. Like many advances in computing, MACSYMA was not an instant hit: Some mathematicians and scientists mistrusted the program's skills at the kind of elaborate symbolic manipulations they required. But the ranks of the converts grew steadily. One was Richard Pavelle, a mathematical researcher who first encountered MACSYMA

in 1973 when he went to work for a defense contracting company that was using MACSYMA in computations concerning the general theory of relativity. As a postdoctoral fellow the year before at the University of Waterloo, Ontario, Pavelle had spent three months working out a single problem of this type, manipulating enormously complex equations by hand. The arduous algebra, normal in this field, did not bother him, but because he had no way of checking the correctness of his result, he had not submitted his findings for publication. When he gained access to the MACSYMA system at his new company, he tried it out on the problem. Two minutes later, the computer's result was ready; it verified his earlier computations, and Pavelle was able to go ahead with the publication of the paper.

Others had similar experiences, and all through the 1970s and 1980s the capabilities of the system were enlarged as users contributed new routines that grew out of their own work. By 1990, according to one estimate, developing and debugging the program had consumed almost 200 person-years of programming time. MACSYMA was then at work in several thousand locations, where innumerable scientists had saved themselves lifetimes of toil. Its thousands of subroutines contained a wealth of mathematical expertise. An astrophysicist could solve problems without knowing or understanding the techniques that the system employed to get an answer. And though the system allowed scientists to explore extremely complex problems that could not be solved in any other way, the very simplest features also endeared it to many users: They found they could use it as an advanced calculator that provided exact answers to ordinary symbolic and numeric problems. True enough, it was a specialist's instrument, of interest only to a small fraction of the scientific community. But like the many thousands of small and large software advances that had preceded it, MACSYMA helped widen the circle of scientists who welcomed the computer as a basic tool in their work. The face of science, experimental and theoretical, had been changed forever.

Tremors
in the Earth

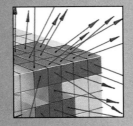

Although few aspects of our planet are less susceptible to direct investigation than the subsurface realm, scientists can extract a wealth of information about the earth from seismic waves—patterns of vibration that ripple through the interior in all directions. Typically generated by earthquakes but also triggered by nuclear explosions or any event forceful enough to shake the ground, these waves of energy are recorded by sensitive detectors called seismometers. The work of organizing the data for study falls to computers.

Seismic waves bend, reflect, change speed and overlap as they make their way through the earth. The distortions are both a curse and a blessing, vastly complicating analysis yet providing valuable clues about the materials through which the waves pass. Before the advent of computers, seismologists were able to solve some of these seismic riddles by developing rudimentary mathematical models of wave behavior. However, the calculations were daunting, and results were imprecise because of the models' simplicity.

The ability of computers to digest mountains of data and render meaningful results in minutes rather than weeks or months has transformed seismology, revealing both the structure of the earth and the actions of earthquakes in remarkable detail. Computers have proved their worth as a tool not only for interpreting data but for collecting it as well; although seismometers still do the initial recording, computers are brought into play right away, automating the information-gathering process and filtering out distortions so that analysis can proceed with little delay.

Seismic data is almost never in short supply. Since the early 1960s, a global network of seismographic stations—originally established to monitor nuclear testing—has been recording tremors all over the world. Seismologists even make their own waves, with small explosive charges or special equipment that thumps the ground, to study specific areas in more detail.

A seismometer detects arriving waves and converts them into an electrical signal; the signal's varying voltages are an analog, or equivalent, of ground motion at the station.

Vibrations caused by an earthquake, an explosion or any force strong enough to shake the ground radiate through the earth and across its surface as seismic waves. When they reach a seismographic station, a combination of devices *(right)* will subject them to a number of transformations.

Signatures of a Seismic Event

Any study of earthquakes or of the earth's interior begins with seismic waves. To get as clear a picture as possible of these waves, seismologists have developed increasingly sophisticated means of recording them. Seismographic stations scattered around the globe now include not only seismometers, which actually detect the patterns of ground motion, but other components that help refine the data and express it in the most useful form.

As shown in the simplified diagram below, seismic waves reaching a station go through a sequence of changes before transmission to a central processing facility. A key step is the conversion of the seismometer's peak-and-valley analog trace into the digital language of computers. Once this is done, computers on the scene can begin to sift through the often-confusing information that seismic waves contain.

By applying an algorithm, or set of problem-solving procedures, the computers can weed out irrelevant signals that the highly sensitive seismometers cannot avoid recording—the rumble of nearby traffic, say, or even the peaceful meanderings of cows through a pasture. Computers at the central station thus receive a clean, legible signature of the event that is to be studied.

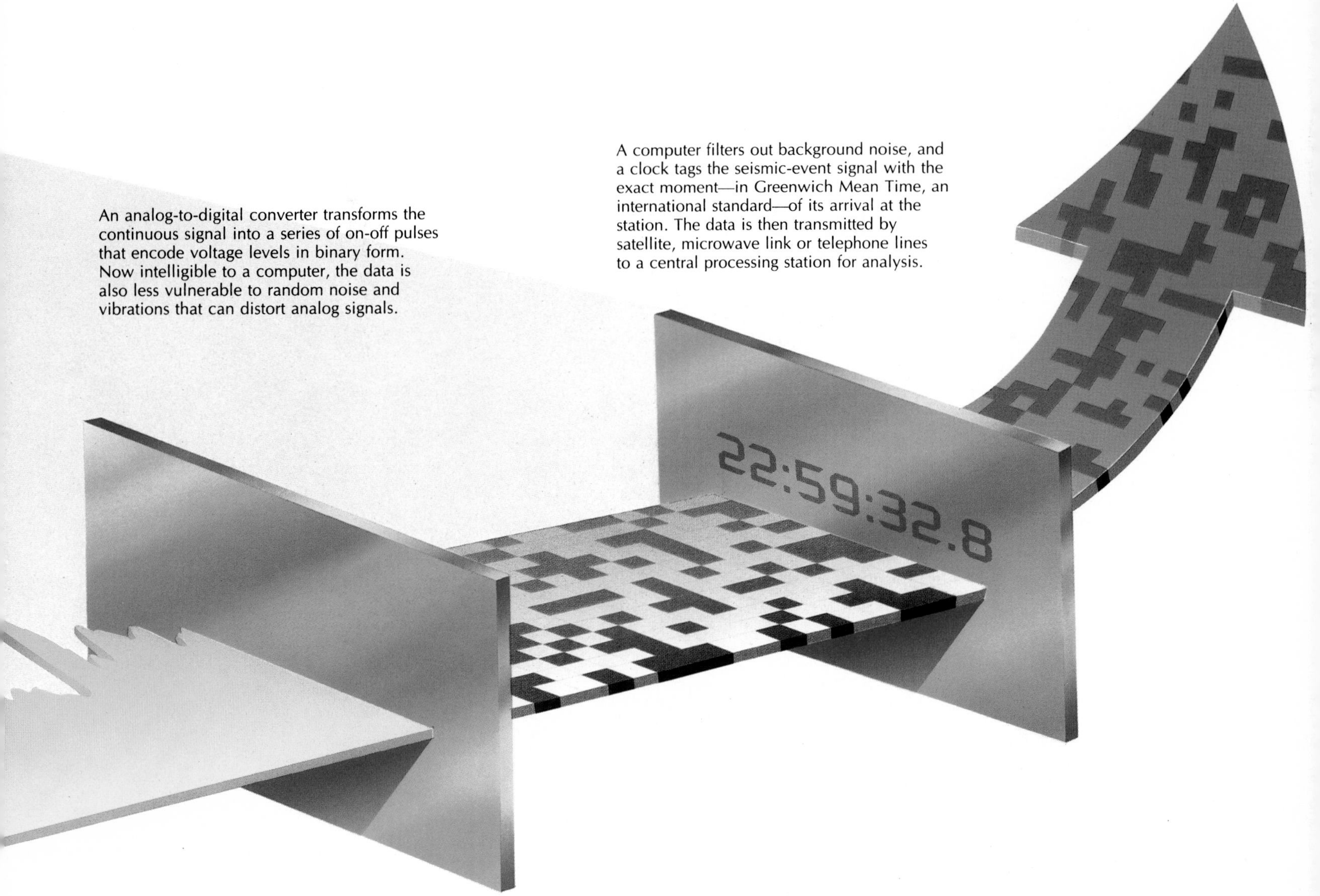

An analog-to-digital converter transforms the continuous signal into a series of on-off pulses that encode voltage levels in binary form. Now intelligible to a computer, the data is also less vulnerable to random noise and vibrations that can distort analog signals.

A computer filters out background noise, and a clock tags the seismic-event signal with the exact moment—in Greenwich Mean Time, an international standard—of its arrival at the station. The data is then transmitted by satellite, microwave link or telephone lines to a central processing station for analysis.

22:59:32.8

Pinpointing the Source of a Tremor

No single recording station can provide enough information about an earthquake to determine where its energy originated—or, for that matter, exactly when. Data from at least four stations is required. The most important detail supplied by each station is arrival time—the instant that a quake's first vibrations were recorded. With arrival times from multiple stations, a computer at a central processing station uses a complex kind of triangulation to work out the latitude, longitude and depth of the fault-rupture that sent shock waves through the planet. The process is a trial-and-error affair: The

computer guesses where and when the quake occurred and calculates hypothetical arrival times for all four stations; it compares the predicted times with the actual ones, compensates for the error and guesses again. This continues until the hypothetical and the actual times match.

Multiple sources of data are also needed to calculate accurately the quake's strength. The computer measures the highest wave peak detected at each station and applies a formula that takes into account the different distances traveled from the epicenter to each station.

Although four stations will yield a reasonably accurate estimate of a quake's origins and magnitude, computers routinely examine data from dozens of stations around the world. In highly active regions with many detectors (below, right), they may churn through hundreds of readings, establishing the epicenter of a quake with an error of only half a kilometer.

22:53:56.5

22:55:34.3

22:57:59.3

22:59:32.8

Squiggles on the computer screen at left represent shock waves from a single earthquake as intercepted by four recording stations. The report from each station begins with the arrival time at the left of the screen and proceeds to display the tremor as each station sensed it. A central station keeps a history of seismic activity throughout the world for retrospective analysis.

The computer can enlarge a portion of a wave to give seismologists a better look at particular patterns of activilty. Such closeup views may lead to a more precise measurement of arrival time by revealing slight tremors in the earth preceding the more intense shaking that triggered a station's clock.

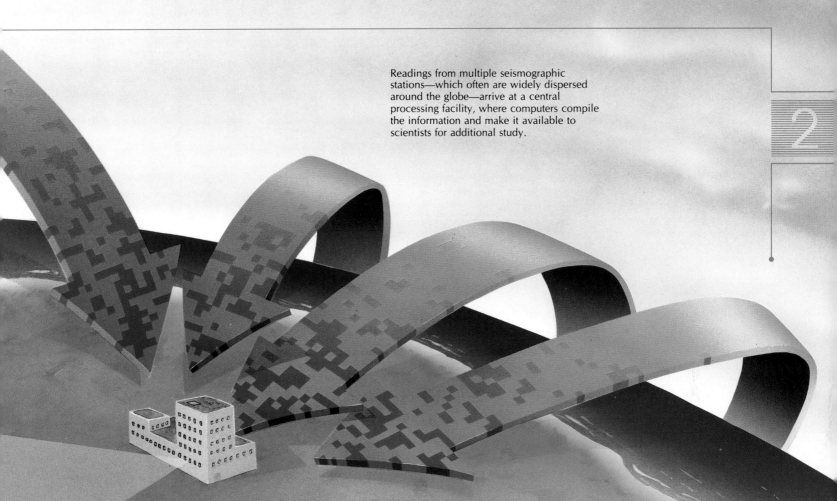

Readings from multiple seismographic stations—which often are widely dispersed around the globe—arrive at a central processing facility, where computers compile the information and make it available to scientists for additional study.

Clustered Detectors Where Quakes Abound

In regions where tremors occur daily, seismologists set up local networks of seismometers tuned to capture a broad range of seismic activity, from inconsequential vibrations to the destructive rumblings of large quakes. Powerful computers process the data and display results almost immediately as a map on computer terminals. In this example, which outlines in red a seismically active region of California, the Long Valley Caldera, detectors appear as three-letter abbreviations. Green lines represent known faults, yellow lines roads. Squares of various sizes indicate quakes of differing magnitudes. Red squares show activity in the last 24 hours, blue ones earlier readings. The computers are programmed to sound an alarm when a sufficiently large tremor is detected or when 20 or more events are detected within an hour.

Probing Earth's Stratified Crust

Among their many seismological services, computers make it possible to map the layered structure of the earth's crust. This profiling is based on a kind of echo sounding. Seismologists detonate small explosive charges to generate seismic waves, then use strings of detectors to record the patterns of reflection that the waves make as they rebound from various subsurface layers, or strata.

Charting underground strata, like pinpointing earthquakes, requires multiple sets of data. Because signals generated by an explosion may be garbled by random noise, reflections from a single blast rarely provide a clear picture. But, as explained below, a series of blasts, positioned to bounce waves against the same subsurface points allows seismologists to isolate reflections from the irregular tracings of noise caused by traffic, construction work or other factors.

In addition to its noise-removal work, a computer is able to gauge the layers' composition by a complex analysis of the timing and strength of the signals. With input from extremely sensitive detectors, a powerful computer can profile the earth in detail to depths as great as 30 miles.

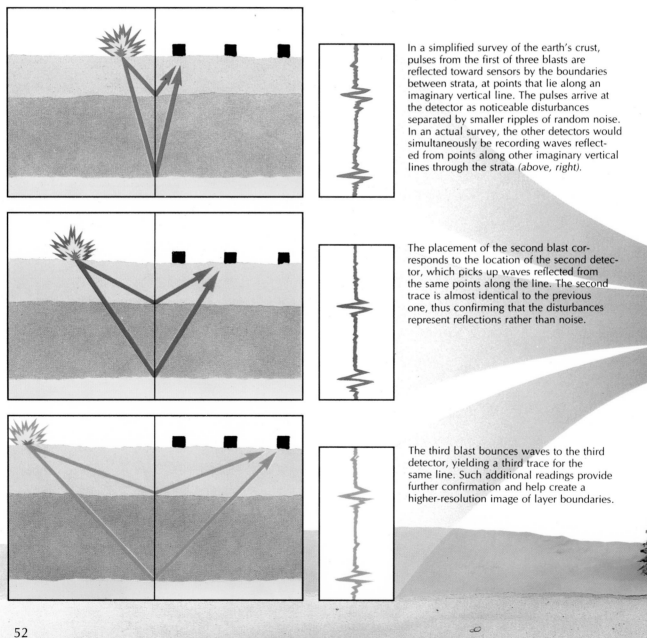

In a simplified survey of the earth's crust, pulses from the first of three blasts are reflected toward sensors by the boundaries between strata, at points that lie along an imaginary vertical line. The pulses arrive at the detector as noticeable disturbances separated by smaller ripples of random noise. In an actual survey, the other detectors would simultaneously be recording waves reflected from points along other imaginary vertical lines through the strata (above, right).

The placement of the second blast corresponds to the location of the second detector, which picks up waves reflected from the same points along the line. The second trace is almost identical to the previous one, thus confirming that the disturbances represent reflections rather than noise.

The third blast bounces waves to the third detector, yielding a third trace for the same line. Such additional readings provide further confirmation and help create a higher-resolution image of layer boundaries.

Seismic waves, radiating at all angles from three explosions, illuminate multiple vertical lines as three detectors register pulses from each blast. Here, waves from two explosions *(red and blue)*, reaching the left and center detectors, supply information about two lines. The third blast *(green)* contributes data about only the left line; an additional detector further to the right would be needed to gather information from this explosion about the other line. A computer combines information from multiple vertical lines into a seismic image of the strata under study *(below, right)*.

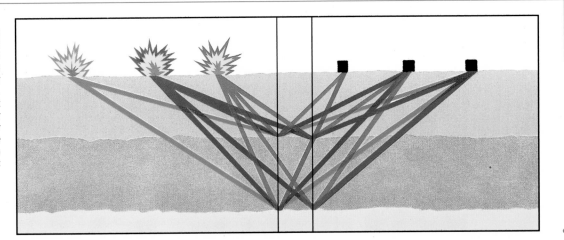

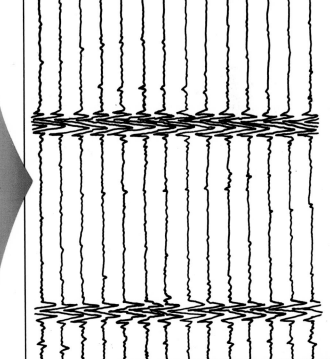

A computer compares seismic traces from all three detectors. It aligns the blast patterns by shifting the second and third traces slightly, compensating for the later arrival of pulses that traveled less direct routes to detectors.

Combining all three traces, the computer produces a single image of wave reflections at both points on the vertical line. Pulses common to all three traces reinforce one another, while random ripples of noise tend to damp one another.

The computer creates a continuous image of strata by displaying traces from many vertical lines. In a real survey, the computer would have displayed readings from many more than the two layers shown here.

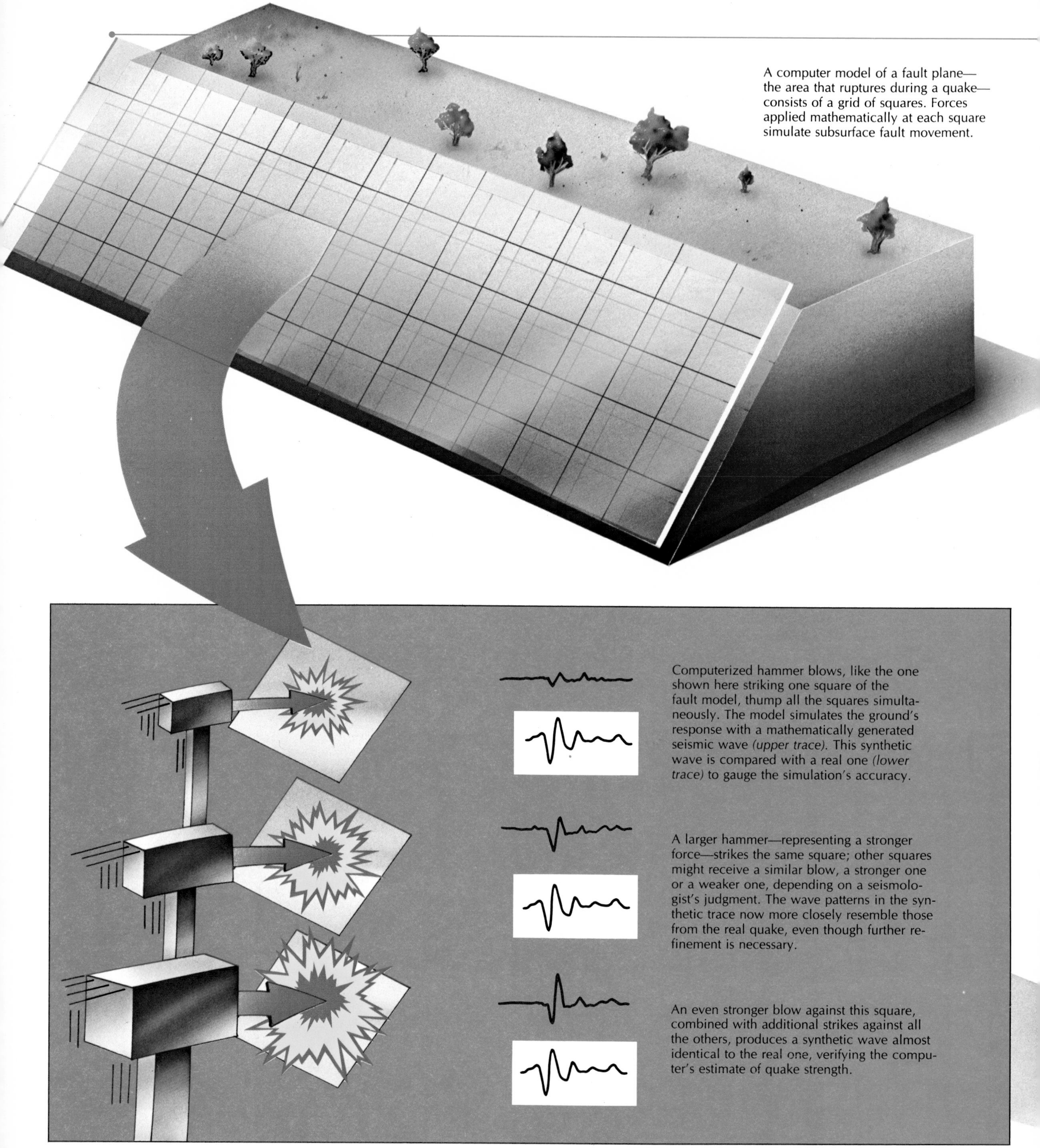

A computer model of a fault plane—the area that ruptures during a quake—consists of a grid of squares. Forces applied mathematically at each square simulate subsurface fault movement.

Computerized hammer blows, like the one shown here striking one square of the fault model, thump all the squares simultaneously. The model simulates the ground's response with a mathematically generated seismic wave *(upper trace)*. This synthetic wave is compared with a real one *(lower trace)* to gauge the simulation's accuracy.

A larger hammer—representing a stronger force—strikes the same square; other squares might receive a similar blow, a stronger one or a weaker one, depending on a seismologist's judgment. The wave patterns in the synthetic trace now more closely resemble those from the real quake, even though further refinement is necessary.

An even stronger blow against this square, combined with additional strikes against all the others, produces a synthetic wave almost identical to the real one, verifying the computer's estimate of quake strength.

Computer Guesswork to Model a Quake

An earthquake occurs when two tectonic plates—gigantic sheets of rock that make up the earth's crust—suddenly break the frictional bond between them and slip in opposite directions. The rupture spreads across the area where the plates meet, called a fault plane, but detectors can measure the seismic effects only at the surface. For a view of the results belowground, seismologists must first create a computer model of the fault plane and the earth around it, derived in part from reflection-profiling data *(pages 52-53)*, then manipulate the model to reconstruct the quake mathematically.

An earthquake can be regarded as the sum of a series of smaller disturbances across the width and breadth of the fault plane. To understand what happened deep within the crust during a quake, seismologists devise a mathematical fault plane consisting of many squares. A computer then simultaneously tests different levels of force at every square—in effect, electronically striking each square with a hammer that varies in size. The model's mathematical earth moves in response, generating synthetic seismic waves that are recorded as if they had actually traveled to detectors on the surface.

By comparing the synthetic waves with real waves recorded during the quake, the computer can evaluate the accuracy of force and slippage estimates. The computer may run through several hundred quake simulations, each time taking into account the influence that a blow against one square exerts against all the others. The guesswork eventually pays off with a simulation that closely resembles the ground's movement along the fault.

Combining the simulated movement of the ground at every square in the fault model, the computer produces a contour map that shows how far different sections of the fault shifted. The measurements are in meters.

A Web of Signals to Map the Interior

Computer modeling on a grand scale helps scientists see deeper than the earth's crustal layers and fault lines. By tracking and timing seismic waves from many years of earthquakes, computers can create three-dimensional images of subterranean regions as far down as the earth's core.

The speed of seismic waves tells a great deal about the regions they penetrate: Waves travel fastest through cold, dense rock and slowest through warmer, less compact rock. To establish the shapes of these regions, a computer combines velocity data from many seismic waves that have passed through the same point. The more waves of diverse origin that pass through a point, the more accurate the density estimate.

Paths of seismic waves crisscross within the earth as they speed from source to detector. By comparing travel times of waves, a computer can determine the characteristics of a specific region *(shaded area)*. The more waves that pass through a region, the more precisely a computer can define its boundaries.

This computer-modeled chunk of the earth's interior shows cold, dense regions as clusters of blue-colored cubes; similar models of the same chunk would use other colors for different temperatures and densities. Blue arrows, which tint a cube as they pass through it, represent waves that travel faster than those of average speed, here indicated by gray arrows.

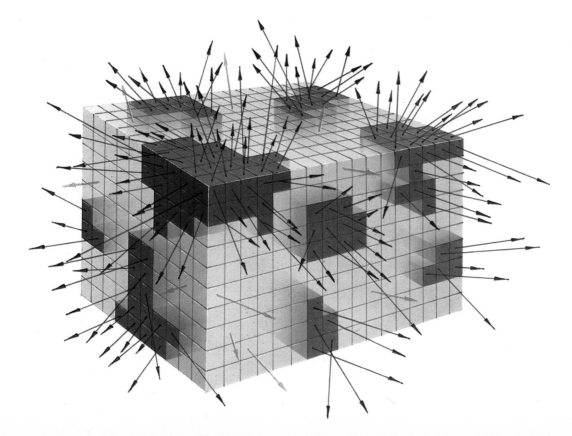

Earth's internal structure, from surface to core, shows up clearly when colored according to temperature and density. The spectrum ranges from violet *(coldest, densest regions)* to red *(warmest, least dense),* with green denoting regions of average values.

Computers
Proliferant

3

To the uninitiated, there was little remarkable about a green squiggle pulsing across a small video screen in a laboratory at the National Institutes of Health, near Washington, D.C. But the portent of the glowing image was so great that scientists in attendance later recalled a sense of elation. Gathered in the laboratory of neurobiologist Arnold Starr in May 1962, they were witnesses to the first unrehearsed demonstration of a revolutionary scientific computer.

Called Linc—it was designed and built at M.I.T.'s Lincoln Laboratory—the machine accomplished the heretofore impossible. It had been programmed to trigger a clicking mechanism at precise intervals. Nearby, a laboratory cat named Jasper lay listening. Electrodes planted in the cat's brain sensed the electrical response of the animal's aural nerves to the sounds impinging on its eardrums and passed the data through a cable to Linc. The machine processed the information and showed the nerve pulses as blips on the monitor, producing the trace of neural activity even as it occurred.

The computer from M.I.T. promised welcome assistance to scientists. For more than a decade, a great variety of automatic data-collection devices—electrodes in a cat's brain, electronic thermometers and the like—had been inundating researchers with more experimental information than they could handle. In the NIH experiment, for instance, it had previously proved impossible, without a computer, to distinguish pertinent data from the thousands of subtly different impulses generated by the cat's nervous system. However, pre-Linc computers were so bulky that they could not be brought into the laboratory and so expensive that they had to be shared by many researchers. Consequently, a computer could be applied to data only after an experiment was complete. It might be days before computed results suggested modifications to the experiment, and scientists could spend as much time awaiting the outcome of a procedure as performing it.

Linc was the first of a wave of small, affordable computers that entered laboratories in the 1960s and 1970s and helped researchers break the data-processing bottleneck. This new hardware, which became less costly and more powerful year by year, was augmented by software that made it easy for scientists to share programs and data and, with a few simple commands, to reconfigure the computer and its software to the demands of a new experiment. During the same period, the scientist's sidekick, the slide rule, became obsolete, replaced by electronic calculators that brought digital speed and accuracy to every computation. Eventually, these gems of miniaturization became computers in their own right. Small enough to fit in a pocket, they had programmable memories that could be adapted to a variety of mathematical tasks.

A MAN OF MANY TALENTS
The individual most responsible for Linc was Wesley Clark, a young computer engineer whose early experience at M.I.T. exposed him to the growing role of electronics in laboratory research. Upon his arrival at the university in 1952, he

joined the Digital Computer Laboratory at the university's Cambridge campus. There he learned programming on the Whirlwind computer, a prototype machine constructed for the U.S. Air Force as the heart of a continental air-defense system. The next year he was introduced to the MTC, another of the lab's computers. He and a colleague used it in an ambitious project to simulate the human nervous system.

When the Digital Computer Laboratory was absorbed by the university's Lincoln Laboratory, a computer research center located 10 miles away in Lexington, Clark went along. Working under Kenneth Olsen, who would soon leave academia to found Digital Electronics Corporation, Clark helped to design the TX-0. This computer and its more powerful successor, the TX-2, were among the first computers made with transistors instead of vacuum tubes. (The TX-1, an intermediate design, was never built.) Both of the machines accepted instructions from a keyboard or from a light-sensitive pen touched against an appropriate spot on the monitor, features that were rare in 1957, when the TX-2 was completed.

Meanwhile, at M.I.T.'s Communications Biophysics Laboratory (CBL), Clark had been participating in seminars on the analysis of electrical signals generated by nerve cells, teaching students and scientists from the biophysics facility how to process neuroelectric data with computers. One of these students, Charles Molnar, proved to be equally talented as an electrical engineer. He and Clark were soon deep in discussions of the important role that computers could play in the biomedical sciences.

With the TX-2 in operation, Clark offered the TX-0, soon to be redundant at Lincoln Lab, to the CBL. To Clark's surprise, Walter Rosenblith, head of the lab, refused the offer. Even though Rosenblith appreciated the contributions that the computer had already made to neuroelectric research, he considered the TX-0 ill suited to his needs. Approximately the size of two refrigerators, the computer could not easily be moved once installed and would become a permanent occupant of scarce laboratory space. In addition, for all the machine's vaunted ease of use, Rosenblith regarded the TX-0 as so much more complex than the other instruments in his laboratory that adopting the computer and teaching staff members to use it might divert the lab from its primary research goals. Clark later recalled Rosenblith's reaction as a valuable lesson: For computers to be welcomed into any laboratory, they would have to become smaller, simpler and more like servants than masters.

DOMESTICATING THE TXs

Clark soon found himself working toward this goal. He and Molnar met with two CBL researchers to discuss the possibility of creating a digital device that would isolate nerve pulses from extraneous electrical activity such as might be generated by muscle movement. Seeing in this need an opportunity to build a computer that Rosenblith would view as a valuable instrument for his laboratory rather than as an electronic albatross around his neck, Clark immediately embraced the project.

To keep things simple, he designed a machine that would incorporate plug-in logic modules designed for the TX-2; but unlike that machine and the TX-0, which could run a variety of different programs, the new one would run only two. One of them would provide an average of the multiple responses measured in a short period of time; the other would produce bar charts, in which each bar would show how many of the responses fell within a specified range of values. And both programs would be wired immutably into the computer's control circuits. Clark named the device ARC, an acronym for "average response computer."

When ARC was completed in early 1958, it included a cathode-ray tube (CRT) display, a plotter and paper-tape punch. The entire system was not much smaller than the TX-0, but the bulk of the computer was made palatable by a unique feature. ARC was portable. That is, it had wheels that permitted the machine to be rolled from one experiment to another. Rosenblith raised no objection to caring for Clark's new creation, and the engineer rode it in triumph through the doorway when it was delivered to CBL. During the course of the next few years, ARC was almost constantly in use, helping researchers to probe the neuroelectrical behavior of the brain. For Clark and Molnar, ARC's popularity was a confirmation of their belief that computers, even those that had limited capability, could do many useful things in a laboratory.

Although Clark had made his point, he was fundamentally dissatisfied with ARC. It was a special-purpose device that had limited utility even for scientists who were working in other areas of biophysics. Clark knew that reprogrammable computers would be much more economical, because a single machine could be tailored to a variety of different experiments. In 1961, he proposed building such a machine for biomedical research, with the stipulation that the new model would be easy to use and not very much more expensive than many other types of laboratory instruments. Clark's suggestion met with a cool response from Lincoln Lab's management, however: The U.S. Air Force was still paying for most of the facility's operations, and applications like Clark's held a low priority.

His immediate boss, Bill Papian, was more encouraging. Papian urged Clark to continue work on his idea and even excused him from his regular duties at the laboratory to do so. After three weeks' sabbatical, Clark returned with a preliminary design for the machine and a set of four basic criteria for the finished product. It should be straightforward to program, simple to maintain, easy to communicate with while operating—so that an experiment could be fine-tuned while under way—and able to process signals directly from lab instruments. Later, he added two more stipulations calculated to ease the computer's way into laboratories. It must cost no more than $25,000—the amount most lab directors could spend without approval from a higher authority. And to keep the new computer from intimidating potential purchasers, it must not be too high for people to see over.

Clark dubbed his design Linc, suggesting its Lincoln Lab roots and punning on the close connection its users would have with their experiments. He began to construct a prototype in late 1961, with Papian's support and a picked team of other engineers and scientists, including Charles Molnar. Assembling the electronic components proved to be relatively easy, because the design was based on commercially available modules that could be put together like building blocks. In addition, the circuitry of the modules was familiar to Clark; the modules were manufactured by DEC, the company founded by Kenneth Olsen, chief architect of the TX-0 and TX-2.

It was the computer's tape drive, intended for storing data and programs, that consumed much of the engineers' time and ingenuity. Clark wanted something much smaller than the tape drives of the day. Users of the TX-2, for instance, shared a single 2,500-foot tape mounted on monstrous reels driven by three-quarter-horsepower motors. The device made so much noise in operation that it often overwhelmed conversation. After months of tinkering, Clark, Molnar and engineer Thomas Stockebrand came up with a comparatively silent drive that recorded experimental observations data on reels of tape small enough to fit into a jacket pocket; a scientist could have a separate store of data for each experiment. Moreover, a tape for each project reduced the likelihood that one researcher might accidentally erase another's data.

A WORKING MODEL
By late February of 1962, the prototype was complete—and still too big. The computer itself now occupied the space of just one refrigerator, but it was connected by 20-foot cables to four boxes, each about the size of an orange crate, that made up the operator's console. One box contained a control panel with switches, indicator lights and control knobs. The second held the monitor, a five-inch video screen adapted from a laboratory oscilloscope (an instrument used to display electrical signals as waves on a cathode ray tube). Two of the new tape transports occupied the third box, while the fourth contained connectors and controls for input and output devices such as laboratory instruments and plotters. Clark later recalled that the Linc team took an upbeat position. They

decided that only the console sections, which could be removed from their boxes and mounted in standard equipment racks, constituted the laboratory instrument. "The rest," Clark said, "was merely the electronics that made it all go and would be tucked out of sight in any convenient closet."

Linc's introduction to the world outside Lincoln Lab was scheduled for April, during a conference in Washington, D.C., on engineering and the life sciences. Clark and Molnar checked Linc into their Washington hotel room with the intention of staging a dress rehearsal for the next day's presentation. But when the machine was turned on, it could not reliably add two and two. The engineers spent a sleepless night on their knees in front of the computer, searching in vain for an elusive fault in the arithmetic unit. Not until the sun came up did they notice a huge broadcast tower outside their window and realize what was wrong: The electromagnetic radiation from the antenna was causing random errors to occur in Linc's perfectly sound hardware.

The computer was promptly rolled from bedroom to conference room. But when zero hour arrived, Molnar was still tinkering, changing program details and testing them. Only as Clark took the podium did Molnar slip him a piece of paper with a message that began: "The following programs have my confidence." Linc performed flawlessly, but Clark and Molnar doubted that the audience fully appreciated the machine's significance. Just one question was asked, by a representative of the Smithsonian Institution. He wanted to know how well the insulation on Linc's wiring would hold up.

FIELD TRIALS

The next day's demonstration, at the National Institutes of Health, evoked a much more enthusiastic response. It was there that Linc had its encounter with Arnold Starr's laboratory pet, Jasper the cat. For months, Starr had been trying to record the electrical signals that carried sound from a cat's ears to its brain. Unfortunately, the faint whispers from nerves were hidden among the much stronger currents generated by movement of the ear drum. On the spot, Molnar wrote a short program for sifting through the signals, and the electrodes were connected to Linc's input channels. In short order, Starr could observe on the monitor the results that had eluded him for so long. "No human being had ever been able to see what we had just witnessed," one of the scientists present later recalled. "It was as if we had the opportunity to ski down a virgin snow field of a previously undiscovered mountain."

The timing of Linc's success was impeccable. NIH had recently formed an advisory committee charged with recommending ways that computers could be used in biomedical studies, and Clark's boss, Bill Papian, served as one of the committee's consultants. Bruce Waxman, executive secretary of the NIH group, was impressed by reports of Linc's performance in Starr's lab. Once, while visiting Lincoln Laboratory in Lexington, he had seen for himself the reliability of the machine's tape unit; Clark had emptied an ashtray filled with cigarette ashes and butts into the drive to demonstrate its immunity to dirt, which all too frequently garbled data stored on the tape drives at NIH. Waxman encouraged Papian and Clark to request an NIH grant to build a Linc for extended testing at the institutes. After the team returned to M.I.T., the idea was expanded to include several computers in different labs having diverse data-processing needs. As the proposal took shape, it became evident that the program would require a grant of about $1.5 million.

But even as Clark, Molnar and the rest of the team set about improving Linc before replicating it, trouble arose at Lincoln Lab. Management there, never enthusiastic about the computer, feared that an expanded project would not fit into the established framework of the organization. The Linc group would therefore have to find another home. Clark's team was stunned when he reported this development—and his own decision to leave Lincoln Lab. He also announced that the computer would henceforth be known, not as Linc, for the lab that had spawned it, but instead as LINC, an acronym for "laboratory instrumentation computer."

For several disheartening months, Clark, Molnar and Papian searched for a suitable base of operations. Then, in late 1962, Walter Rosenblith of the Communications Biophysics Laboratory came to the rescue. He proposed that several New England universities form a consortium to be called the Center for Computer Technology and Research in the Biomedical Sciences. It would have its headquarters at M.I.T. in Cambridge. The first step would be the establishment of a

Improved Computing Tools for the Lab

The history of scientific computing machines is a tale of increasing capability and diminishing size. As computer designers learned to pack in more power per cubic inch, their products became commonplace in the laboratory, where they eased the researcher's burden by automatically collecting data, controlling experiments and processing results.

Further advances in miniaturization fueled the demand for faster and more powerful computers and spurred the development of computer-like calculators. Desktop models came first, but they were soon followed by hand-held devices *(page 66)* that gave scientists and engineers the power of computation to tackle complex calculations formerly requiring a full-fledged computer for solutions.

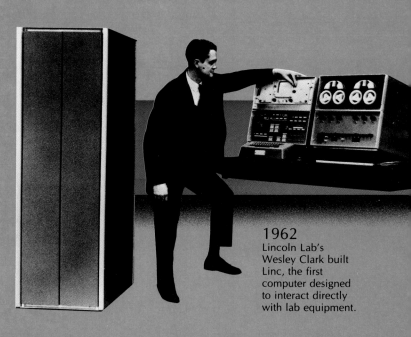

1962
Lincoln Lab's Wesley Clark built Linc, the first computer designed to interact directly with lab equipment.

Center Development Office (CDO), which would work out the organizational details among the various universities and look for sources of financial support. The LINC team, Rosenblith suggested, would immediately be adopted by the development office so that the team could finish redesigning the computer and continue its effort to spread the technology into laboratories across the country as rapidly as possible.

The proposal was accepted almost at once. Rosenblith was named director of CDO, with Papian as associate director. In January 1963, all the staff and equipment from Lincoln Lab's biomedical computer operation arrived at the development office's new Cambridge quarters, where they were joined by several members of CBL. Bruce Waxman, in what Clark later called "a dazzling display of civil service at its best," quickly put together the $1.5-million grant, drawing half from NIH funds and half from a newly established bioscience program at the National Aeronautics and Space Administration. The money was earmarked for the construction and evaluation of 16 LINCs, four to remain with the parent group in Cambridge and 12 to be assigned to research teams chosen by a nationally constituted board.

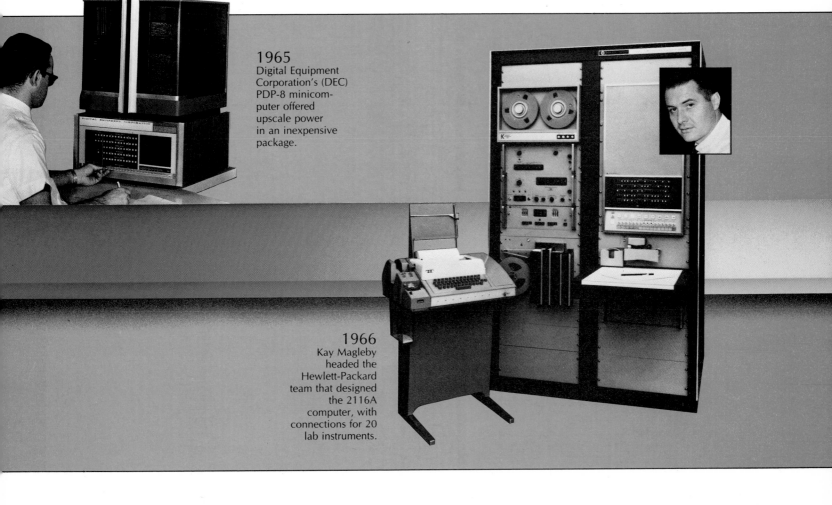

1965
Digital Equipment Corporation's (DEC) PDP-8 minicomputer offered upscale power in an inexpensive package.

1966
Kay Magleby headed the Hewlett-Packard team that designed the 2116A computer, with connections for 20 lab instruments.

There was to be no charge for the computers, but they were not quite free. Molnar suggested, partly in jest, that the winners in the competition should put together their own machines when they came to Cambridge for orientation. Clark took the idea more seriously than his colleague had proposed it. He saw immediately that he could reduce assembly costs and, at the same time, teach the scientists how to operate and maintain the machines in their own laboratories. At once, the team began preparing LINC kits for the workshops, which were scheduled for the summer of 1963.

When the first group of computer novices arrived in Cambridge on July 1 (some of them carrying golf clubs that they would never get to use), Clark and his technicians were still scrambling to finish the kits. Other members of the team waged a holding action until they were ready, conducting a two-week crash course on the theory and use of computers. When the assembly work got under way, the visiting scientists proved enthusiastic. Long days and nights were common, and meals at Fox and Tishman's Restaurant in nearby Kendall Square were punctuated by discussions of computer technology. In just two weeks, the machines were ready. As a final assignment, each visiting team prepared and ran

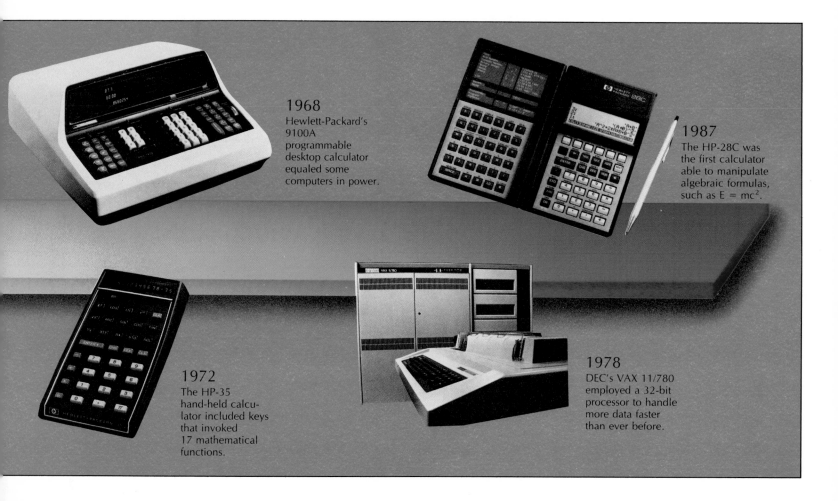

1968
Hewlett-Packard's 9100A programmable desktop calculator equaled some computers in power.

1987
The HP-28C was the first calculator able to manipulate algebraic formulas, such as $E = mc^2$.

1972
The HP-35 hand-held calculator included keys that invoked 17 mathematical functions.

1978
DEC's VAX 11/780 employed a 32-bit processor to handle more data faster than ever before.

a program of the type that it would use in its laboratory. Then hosts and guests repaired to the F and T, as they now fondly knew the restaurant, for an exuberant farewell banquet. Three days later, the next set of neophytes showed up, and the cycle began all over again.

By mid-September, all 12 LINCs had been assembled and installed in laboratories around the United States. They were quickly put to work. One group of researchers applied its computer to the study of blood-flow hydrodynamics and the behavior of heart muscles. Another LINC helped to analyze the genes of bacteria. And one team, investigating communication between humans and dolphins, encountered a unique equipment hazard: Their subject, a dolphin named Elvar, could accurately spurt a potentially short-circuiting stream of sea water a distance of 20 feet.

At the close of the evaluation program in March 1965, the 12 LINCs had amassed 50,000 hours of operating time, and most of the scientists reported significant results in their work. At $32,000 each, the computers had cost the program more than Clark had hoped, but other scientists were willing to pay the price to get LINCs for themselves. In September 1964, commercial production of the machines was turned over to DEC, the manufacturer of the digital modules. In the next 20 years, DEC built some 1,200 computers based on the original LINC design. They became mainstays in large and small scientific facilities around the world. But perhaps LINC's most important contribution was the excitement it engendered by opening new doors for researchers. It had produced, in the words of the evaluation committee's report, "an aura of adventure that one finds rarely in academic and scientific pursuits."

THE AGE OF THE MINICOMPUTER

By the time DEC took over production of LINC, the company was a rapidly growing computer manufacturer in its own right, having discovered a niche in the computer market for relatively small machines with features like the ones that the firm's founder, Kenneth Olsen, had built into the TX-0 at Lincoln Lab. Beginning with the PDP-1 in 1959, DEC came out with a succession of computers, and almost every one was smaller, more powerful and less expensive than its predecessor. Then, in 1965, the company introduced a machine that would consolidate the revolution that LINC had begun. The PDP-8, approximately the size of LINC, was more powerful, and it broke Wesley Clark's price barrier: It cost only $18,000. In the next two decades, more than 100,000 units of the original PDP-8 and variants were built, most going to work in scientific settings around the world.

The commercial success of the PDP-8 lured a number of competitors into the race to sell these machines—called minicomputers to distinguish them from larger, more expensive mainframes. Hewlett-Packard was an early entrant. No Johnny-come-lately to scientific research, the California firm had been building laboratory instruments since its birth in 1938. Established in a garage behind a rented house, it had grown into a multinational corporation with billions of dollars in sales annually.

William Hewlett and David Packard had become close friends while both were students of engineering at Stanford University. As part of his thesis, Hewlett designed a new type of audio oscillator, an electronic instrument that generates sound at precise frequencies for use in testing audio equipment. The instrument promised to outdo existing oscillators in price, size and performance. After graduating in 1938, the two engineers formed a partnership to build and sell their invention, which they named the Model 200A "because the number sounded big." The entrepreneurs took over the Packards' one-car garage as a workshop and mailed descriptions of the oscillator to prospective customers. A few orders trickled in, along with a letter from Walt Disney Studios. The animated-film maker sought an oscillator, but the studio technicians were looking for one with characteristics different from those of the 200A. Disney's specifications proved easy to meet. A quick redesign led to the Model 200B and to the fledgling firm's first volume order: The Disney people purchased eight of the devices, which were used in developing the sound track for the animated epic *Fantasia*.

In the first year, sales totaled about five thousand dollars. Frederick Terman, a friend and former professor, recalled the way he could tell how the partners were doing. "If Packard's car was in the garage, it meant they had no orders. But if it was out in the street, they had some business and were hard at work soldering, wiring, painting—you name it." The manufacture of the oscillators even spilled into the Packards' kitchen, where the oven served to bake gray paint onto the steel instrument cabinets. By 1940, however, modest success allowed the partners to hire their first employees and set up operations in the rear half of a small store. The company soon outgrew these quarters and built its own plant in 1942. By 1950, the firm had 200 employees, 70 products—mostly measuring instruments—and annual sales of two million dollars.

One of the company's biggest research advantages was a phenomenon that later became known as the "next bench syndrome." Products were often developed, refined and evaluated on the basis of what "the guy at the next bench" needed for his work. Since most of Hewlett-Packard's customers shared the needs of the company's own scientists and engineers, those serendipitous products often found a lucrative market. Consequently, HP, as the company was widely known, developed an adaptability and feel for the scientific-instrument marketplace that was hard for competitors to match.

The environment at HP was made to order for engineer Kay Magleby, who

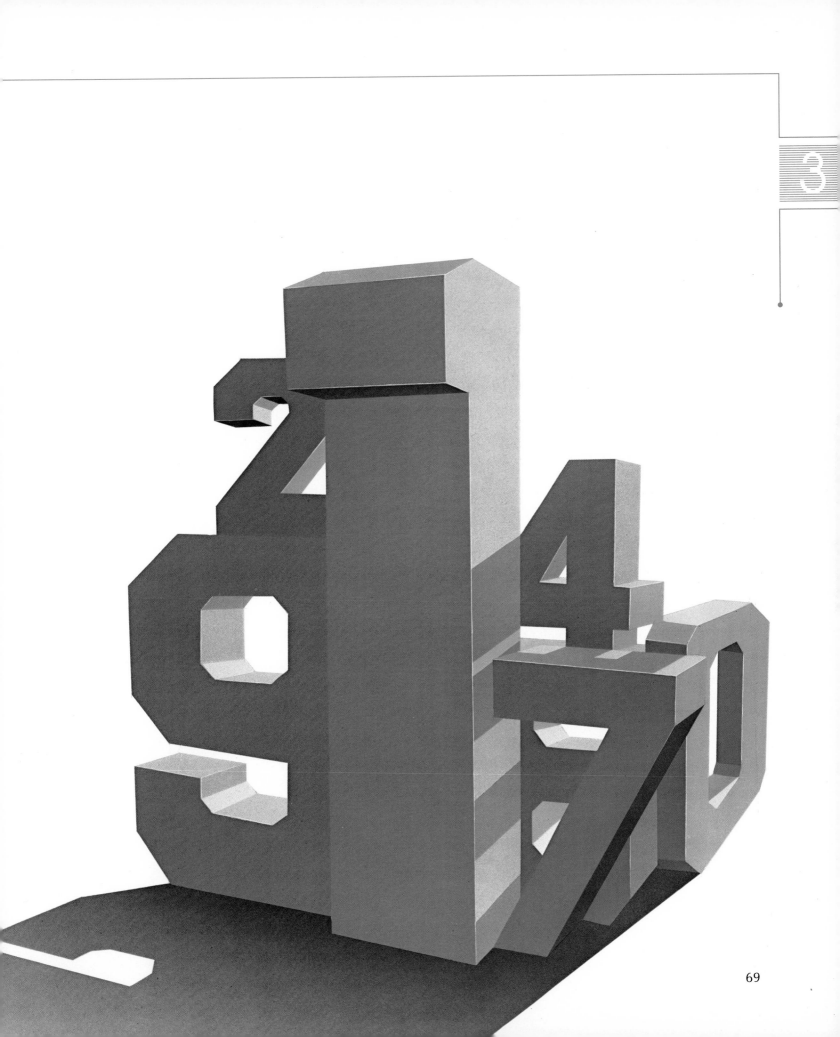

would parlay a long-standing fascination with computers into a new product line for the company. Magleby's early computer experience came in 1957 while he was still an undergraduate at the University of Utah in Salt Lake City. Smitten by the machines, he enrolled in every course that taught the design and use of computers, and he spent many of his free hours working with the primitive machines then available at the university. Shortly after completing his undergraduate work in 1958, Magleby joined Hewlett-Packard in Palo Alto, attracted by a demanding program that combined full-time employment with graduate courses in computer science at nearby Stanford University. Much to his disappointment, however, his new job had nothing to do with computers; instead, he was put to work designing oscilloscopes.

In 1963, events turned in his favor. The oscilloscope division moved to Colorado Springs, and Magleby, by then just finishing his Ph.D. thesis, was unwilling to follow. Instead he arranged a transfer to HP's central research lab, where he was to develop ways of adding computer technology to instruments. To help himself in the work, Magleby requisitioned the best laboratory computer available at the time, a DEC PDP-5. He soon discovered that to connect an instrument to the computer, he first had to custom-design a plug and socket for it. Then he had to write software that would accept data from the instrument. From the point of view of the guy at the next bench, Magleby thought, the effort required to incorporate the DEC computer into experimental systems was just too arduous. So Magleby decided to design a computer of his own that would be much easier to use. He took the idea to Paul Stoft, the manager of the lab, who told him to go ahead.

A short time later, Bill Hewlett, who liked to keep in touch with the research staff, happened by the lab and asked Stoft what Magleby was up to. The answer surprised Hewlett, Stoft later recalled. "After all, we weren't in the computer business." But Stoft and Magleby were able to convince Hewlett that an HP-designed computer would be a natural extension of the company's product line, which by now included printers and plotters for computers, as well as various kinds of laboratory instruments. Magleby was invited to present the idea to the firm's executive committee, which voted not only to approve the project but also to expand its staff. By 1965, the computer project had grown to such a size that Hewlett placed Magleby in charge of it and transferred the work out of the central research lab.

A year and a half after the move, Magleby's team completed the most complex product-development effort in HP's history. The Model 2116A computer was introduced in November of 1966. It could do everything that an ordinary minicomputer could, but its real value lay in its new features. It was the first computer specifically designed for the sometimes harsh working environment found in laboratories. The 2116A could function in temperatures ranging from 32° F. to 131° F., in humidity up to 95 percent, and it could tolerate wide fluctuations in the voltage and in the frequency of its electrical supply. It could also withstand vibration and was shielded against electromagnetic interference of the kind that had almost ruined LINC's debut. Twenty standard HP instruments could be plugged into the computer without modifying the hardware or producing custom-written software.

Priced at about $47,000, the new computer was an immediate success, starting a whole new line of business for Hewlett-Packard. By 1970, with computer sales of $65 million, the company was second only to DEC in the minicomputer market. In the meantime, however, another product was emerging from the central research lab that would have an even greater impact on HP's profits—and that within a decade would change the computing habits of practically every scientist.

SETTING OUT IN A NEW DIRECTION

Paul Stoft, left out of the action when Magleby took charge of the computer team in 1965, had soon found a new project to shepherd. In late summer of that year, two hopeful inventors had approached Hewlett-Packard with working prototypes of a new device, the electronic calculator.

One of the calculators incorporated an algorithm devised by engineer Malcolm McMillan that endowed the machine with a unique capability. In mathematics, values for certain expressions, essential to the solution of many engineering problems, cannot be found by addition, subtraction, multiplication or division. Mathematicians called these expressions transcendental functions and consulted tables for their values, as did even large computers of the early 1960s. McMillan's algorithm enabled his device to calculate the values of the most common transcendentals, such as logarithms and trigonometric functions. Unfortunately, the device was slow, taking several seconds to complete just one of the special calculations. Worse, the calculator could not handle extremely large numbers in a problem that also contained very small ones, as happens often in fields such as nuclear physics.

The second prototype, built inside a green balsa-wood box by an engineer named Tom Osborne, could not solve transcendental expressions. However, innovative electronic circuitry endowed the calculator with blazing speed, and it could handle numbers of any size.

Hewlett-Packard engineers were quick to see the appeal of a calculator that combined the strengths of these two prototypes. Scientists would be able to get fast, accurate answers to mathematical problems that arose in their daily work. At the time, these answers could be produced only by slide rule or by computer. The slide-rule approach was tedious, and there were often long queues of scientists waiting for a turn at the computers. The company bought the rights to both men's ideas, hired Tom Osborne as a consultant and gave to Paul Stoft the responsibility for developing a marketable product.

The task was at least as difficult as designing a computer. Many of the engineers who worked on the project insisted that they were in fact designing a computer—a special-purpose machine, with a great deal of programming built into the hardware. This firmware, as it came to be called, made available a wide selection of specialized mathematical functions at the touch of special keys arrayed along the sides of the calculator's slanting face. Other keys permitted sequences of calculations to be programmed into the machine's modest memory, then executed repeatedly. A magnetic recorder allowed programs in memory to be stored on a specially coated plastic wafer the size of a credit card; the recorder also transferred programs stored on such cards into memory for use. Scientists thus could build a library of frequently used programs to share with colleagues. Introduced in 1968 as the Model 9100A, the calculator was a 40-pound desktop machine, approximately the size of a breadbox. It sold for about $4,900 and was more capable mathematically than some general-purpose computers costing thousands of dollars more.

THE INCREDIBLE SHRINKING CALCULATOR

The 9100A had a great fan in Bill Hewlett, who liked almost everything about the new product except its bulk. The cofounder of HP believed that his company should be able to shrink the machine enough to be held in the hand. In the fall of 1970, that goal began to seem attainable. Hewlett-Packard's research and development team had been investigating a new development in electronic miniaturization, the integrated circuit. This recent invention crammed thousands of transistors onto a silicon chip no larger than a soda cracker. It seemed likely that most of the 9100A's features could be squeezed onto a few integrated circuits and packed into a box only slightly bigger than the hand-held "four bangers"—they could add, subtract, multiply and divide—that the new technology had already brought to market.

Convinced that fast action was essential to beat other manufacturers to market with a more sophisticated device, Hewlett put a development team to work immediately. The assignment was to produce the HP-35, a scientific calculator. It was to fit in a pocket, to run for four hours between battery recharges, to handle many of the jobs that a 9100A could, and to bear a price that any laboratory— and many individuals—could afford.

Because size was an overriding consideration, the engineers first designed the box. To fit the calculator's 35 keys in a space smaller than an index card, the designers placed them closer together than the industry standard, then shrank them to compensate. So that one key would not be mistaken for another, the keys were color coded and clearly marked with the function that each controlled. And since HP had a mass market in mind, esthetic concerns played a much larger role than usual. The case was sculpted to look thinner than it really was. Sitting on a desk, it appeared to float.

Once the question of the exterior design was settled, the necessary electronics had to be squeezed inside: five integrated circuits, each of which was the equivalent of hundreds of transistors; three permanent memory chips, which held the firmware; a variety of customized circuits; and an array of light-emitting diodes (LEDs) that had built-in magnifying lenses for displaying both input and results as one-quarter-inch numbers and letters. In addition, space had to be reserved for the rechargeable nickel-cadmium batteries that would be necessary to power the device.

The HP-35 was released in January 1972, billed as an "electronic slide rule." Weighing in at nine ounces, it was a marvel of miniaturization; and priced at $395, it became the first product that Hewlett-Packard had ever sold through retail stores and by direct mail. In the first year alone, 100,000 HP-35s were purchased—10 times the number that HP had hoped to sell. Buyers, who ranged from civil engineers to ship navigators, were attracted by an unparalleled combination of speed and precision in a tiny package. In one typical trial, a skilled engineer working with a slide rule took five minutes to find the great-circle distance between Miami and San Francisco: 2,255 miles. Another engineer working with an HP-35 required only 65 seconds to solve the same problem.

Hewlett would later boast, "Never has a major computational device, in this case the slide rule, been so quickly and completely supplanted by the introduction of a modern technology."

As it turned out, competition for Hewlett-Packard in the calculator market took a long time to materialize. Two years passed before a comparable product emerged, and during that period, HP made about $115 million from sales of the HP-35 and its derivatives. When competition at last heated up in 1974, Hewlett-Packard was ready to leapfrog the opposition with the HP-65, the first programmable pocket calculator. It combined the convenience, portability and personal touch of the HP-35 with the flexibility and power of the old 9100A. And like its predecessors, it helped change the scientific world. Computing power that had once required a roomful of electronics could now be held in one hand and programmed with the other.

TAMING THE OPERATING SYSTEM

The integrated circuits and other electronic advances that HP used to such great advantage in its calculators showed up in bigger machines as well. By the 1970s, many companies had incorporated them in powerful minicomputers that pervaded scientific facilities around the world. A single machine might be employed at different times by dozens of people, for everything from running and analyzing experiments to formating results and printing reports. Some computers could even serve several people at once, through a technique called time-sharing. The software of the day, however, often failed to measure up to the hardware. Too many computers were burdened with cumbersome operating systems. These programs interpret commands and tell the computer how to respond. An operating system manages the storage of data and programs; it provides access to peripheral equipment such as lab instruments, video screens and printers; and in the case of time-sharing, it allocates thin slices of computing time to each user in accordance with predetermined priorities.

Manufacturers usually equipped each type of computer with a customized operating system. Few were easy to learn or use, and many had structural quirks that reflected the design of the machines they governed. A scientist exposed to an unfamiliar computer often had to learn a new set of commands. Worse, since programs for experimental control and analysis were tailored to the system they ran on, a researcher who changed computers might have to purchase or rewrite an entire library of software. More often than not, learning to handle a computer got in the way of using it productively.

This situation was dramatically altered in the mid-1970s by the emergence of a new operating system that was easy to use and adaptable to almost any minicomputer. The programs originated at AT&T's Bell Labs in New Jersey, as a side effect of a cooperative venture between AT&T, General Electric and M.I.T. to produce a time-sharing operating system. The result of that effort, called Multics, had two significant disadvantages: It was slow in responding to commands and it was greedy for expensive memory space. Bell Labs decided to back out of the project in 1969, and the programming research group gave up the General Electric GE 645 computer that had been acquired to do the work with Multics. Loss of the time-sharing machine distressed programmer Ken Thompson. He held no soft feelings for Multics, but he enjoyed using the GE 645

The UNIX Approach to Running a Computer

In the early days of computers, instructing one of the machines to perform the most common tasks, such as storing data in memory, required detailed knowledge of the circuitry. To make computers easier to use, their designers evolved the idea of an operating system—a collection of software that accomplishes frequently recurring chores, whether printing information, conveying it to a magnetic disk, or displaying it on a terminal. One operating system, called UNIX, is particularly effective at simplifying the use of computers. It has become a favorite of scientists, and several of its key features have been widely adopted.

In UNIX, two layers of software—the shell and the kernel—permit scientists to create complex data-processing procedures merely by stringing together simple commands (pages 76-77). UNIX's filing strategy adds to the operating system's appeal. The kernel provides a storage structure for individual program and data files so that related files can be grouped into directories and subdirectories. The hierarchical arrangement resembles an upside-down tree, with the trunk as the system's main directory and other directories branching below. This approach to filing makes stored data and programs easier to locate and helps users organize their work.

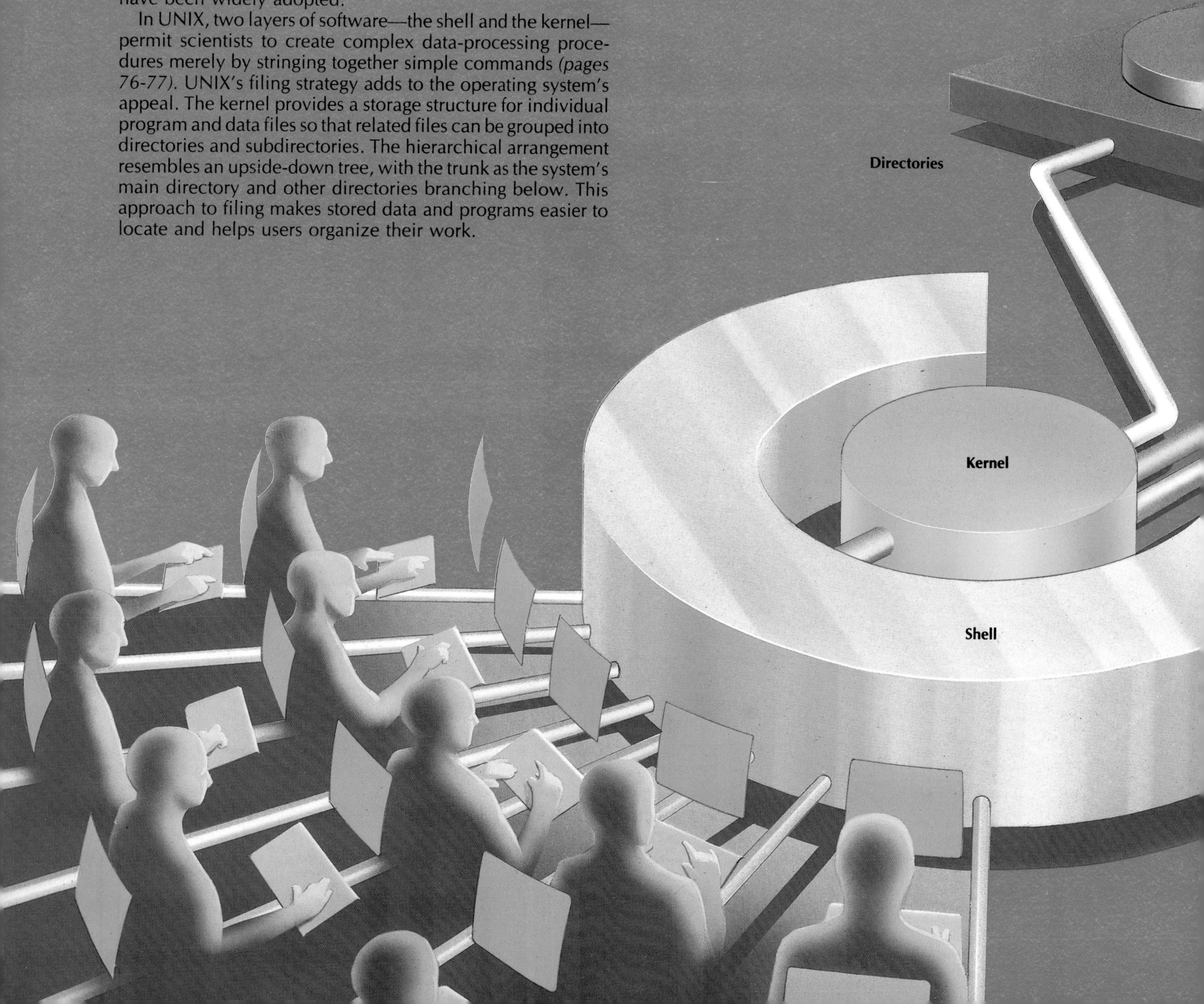

Directories

Kernel

Shell

UNIX organizes elements in the computing process into three categories. Directories are listings of file names in hierarchical groupings that provide ready access to stored data. Program and data files hold the actual information to be processed—the results of an experiment, for example, or the sequence of instructions that make up a program. Input and output devices—lab equipment and computer keyboards as well as printers, monitors and data-storage devices—also fall under the kernel's control.

Programs and Data

Input and Output

Access to a computer's resources is shared through UNIX's two layers of software *(left)*. The shell, which provides a set of simple commands, facilitates dialogue with the machine. The kernel, in arranging for the execution of instructions received through the shell, manages the computer and its equipment, as well as the storage and retrieval of data and program files *(above)*.

Multiple Ways to Handle Data

In an example of a typical lab experiment, a probe measures the fluctuating temperature of a chemical solution. The scientist has directed the probe's output—the temperature readings —to the input channel of a program named CAPTURE, which accepts readings at discrete intervals and time-stamps each one. The resulting data then flows to CAPTURE's standard output device—a monitor, perhaps, or a storage disk—unless, as here, it is redirected to another program's input channel.

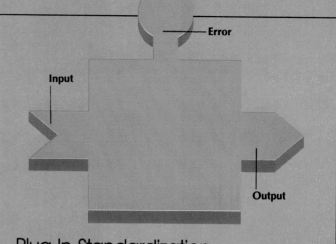

Plug-In Standardization

UNIX building-block programs must be written so that each accepts input from all the others, a degree of compatibility that permits linking modules together, output to input. A standardized output path for error messages prevents them from corrupting the experimental data being processed by the program.

CAPTURE

AVERAGE

AVERAGE

CONVERT

A more complex analysis—charting temperature change over time—might involve linking four program blocks. As above, the AVERAGE program receives input from CAPTURE, but now the output is channeled to CONVERT, where Fahrenheit readings are changed to Celsius. The data then flows to SCALE, which prepares the information to be displayed in graph form with temperature on the vertical axis and time on the horizontal axis. Finally, the data is processed by PLOT, which guides a plotter in drawing the chart.

UNIX is popular among researchers for its simple, building-block method of computerizing experimental procedures. The operating system includes scores of small, individual programs, each performing a specific function. Others can be added as desired. Activating a program requires little more than typing its name. Moreover, it is easy to combine programs in a variety of ways to serve a wide range of purposes.

Versatility of this degree depends on rigid standardization among the individual blocks *(left)*. Compatibility between building blocks permits linking them together and sending the chain's end product to a monitor, a printer or any other output device connected to the computer. Accomplishing all this is no more difficult than typing the name of the programs in the order they are to be used, concluding with the output device. Furthermore, a researcher can assign a name to this chain of events and store it away for future use.

To organize the temperature data, the scientist merely types in the names of additional programs, in this case AVERAGE and SORT. UNIX would then route CAPTURE's output through the first of these building blocks, a program that averages temperature readings in groups of three, and on to SORT, which arranges the averages in descending numerical order. Because SORT's standard output is the computer screen, the organized list appears there automatically.

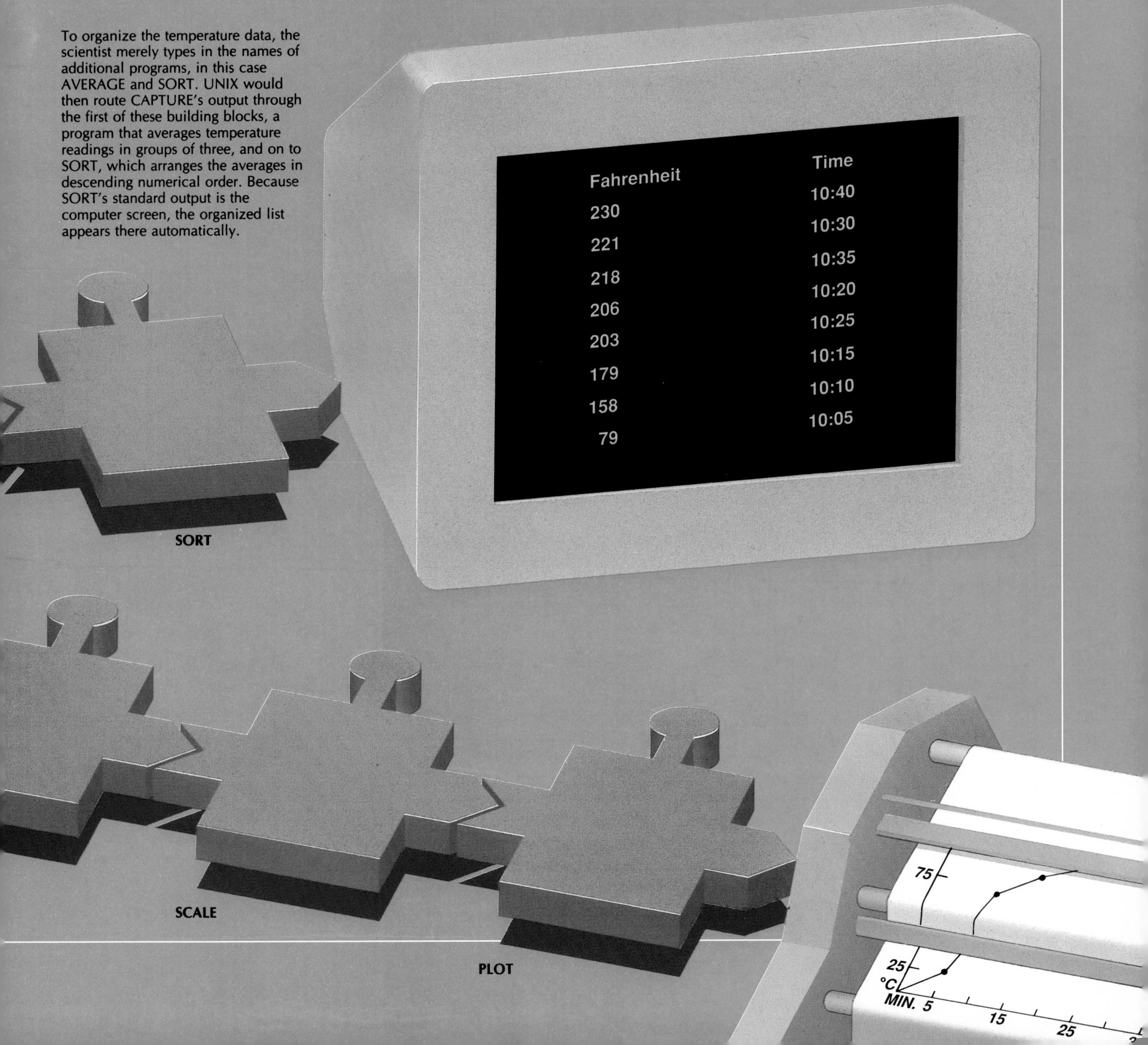

Fahrenheit	Time
	10:40
230	10:30
221	10:35
218	10:20
206	10:25
203	10:15
179	10:10
158	10:05
79	

SORT

SCALE

PLOT

75

25
°C
MIN. 5   15   25

to run a program he had written, a simulation of the solar system that he called Space Travel. Casting about the laboratory for a substitute computer, he came upon a seldom-used PDP-7, which was obsolescent barely five years after it had been released by DEC.

To Thompson's delight, the old machine was far superior to the GE 645 in its graphic display, which made Space Travel much more satisfying to watch. But as he began the job of rewriting the simulation to operate in the PDP-7, he found that the computer lacked the utility programs, commonly part of an operating system, that automate such chores as copying files and printing out program listings. Utilities were the tools of Thompson's software trade; by taking over mundane tasks and duties, they freed him to focus on the creativity of programming. Missing these implements, Thompson began to write some of them himself in PDP-7 assembly language. He also put together a file-management system, software that the computer used to keep, store and retrieve data.

Although Thompson was tailoring his programs to an outmoded computer, word of his progress trickled through Bell Labs, attracting the curious among the organization's programmers. One named Dennis Ritchie joined forces with Thompson, and together the two men began to develop a full-fledged operating system that would incorporate a complete set of utilities and an expanded file-management system. Hampered by the limited power and memory of the PDP-7, they petitioned management for a more advanced computer. At first their efforts were in vain. Eventually, however, the system's spreading reputation within Bell Labs—and the politically astute addition of some text-editing features attractive to another department—led to the purchase of a PDP-11, DEC's recently introduced minicomputer. Before long, Thompson and Ritchie had converted the system to run on the new machine, and Bell Labs, having in the meantime bought several more PDP-11s, found that researchers preferred the homegrown operating system to the software supplied with the machines by DEC. The two programmers put together a manual in 1971 to help newcomers learn the system, which they had dubbed UNIX, a play on the word Multics, reflecting the new operating system's single-user orientation.

A second edition of the manual appeared in June 1972. It outlined all the significant features of UNIX, which had by then fully matured into a system that supported time-sharing much more efficiently than had Multics. At that time, UNIX comprised more than 100 modular programs. Each could be invoked, by typing its name, to carry out a limited task, such as recording instrument readings or sorting data. Program names were easily linked into chains that performed new functions. When a new program was written, it would become a permanent addition to the UNIX software library, and would thus be freely available to others.

So far, Thompson and Ritchie had composed all the UNIX programs in assembly language. Doing so ensured software that would demand as little memory as possible and operate speedily. But writing the programs in this form made adding to the UNIX library a challenging business and excluded all but the most expert programmers from the work of developing software. For these reasons, UNIX's creators decided in 1973 to rewrite all but the central kernel that tied the operating system to the PDP-11's central processing unit. For this modification, they selected a high-level programming language that they had developed. It was named C (a successor to a language called B, itself derived from BCPL, Basic Combined Programming Language). Like most such languages, C allowed programmers to express their commands to the computer in words and recognizable symbols rather than the numbers and letters of assembly language. A program called a compiler translated this script directly into the ones and zeros that computers comprehend.

In July 1974, the C version of UNIX was described in a magazine for computer professionals; this was the first time the system was presented to a large audience outside Bell Labs. UNIX fared just as well in that wider world as it had in its birthplace, in part because of its close association with the PDP-11. The fast, flexible and, at a price of $50,000, relatively inexpensive computer was in wide use by then, only four years after it had appeared on the market in 1970.

University science departments found this already attractive machine even more enticing when AT&T decided to license UNIX to educational institutions for a nominal fee. In a typical chemistry department, a PDP-11 equipped with UNIX could manage program and data files for dozens of students and professors; provide straightforward control over a variety of laboratory equipment; allow researchers to share and combine their programs easily; and furnish text-editing and data-formating capabilities for the preparation of reports. UNIX was also well suited to computer education because of the easy access it gave to programming tools. By 1983, eighty percent of colleges granting computer-science degrees had adopted UNIX; anyone studying computers was virtually guaranteed to come in contact with the system.

FROM SCHOOLS TO WORK
Students who became familiar with UNIX were eager to carry it to the jobs they took after graduation. And in many cases they could do so, even if there was no PDP-11 available. Because UNIX had been rewritten in C, the operating system could be adapted to any computer for which a C compiler had been written. Computer manufacturers, aware of UNIX's growing appeal, willingly undertook the few months' work required to rewrite the assembly-language kernel for their new machines. This ability to operate many kinds of equipment helped make UNIX a nearly universal standard.

The operating system's dominance was further cemented in 1980, when a new version, with many novel features, was released by a software development group at the University of California at Berkeley. Although it was intended for use on all kinds of computers, the new version got a boost from the popularity of another DEC computer, the VAX 11/780. Introduced in 1978, the VAX was designed to have nearly immediate access to 4.3 gigabytes of storage—the equivalent of more than two million pages like this one, and hundreds of times the capacity of ordinary minicomputers. Even though no VAX was actually equipped with so much memory, the machine was far more powerful than the PDP-11. Because a VAX could run much of the existing PDP-11 software, it quickly supplanted the older machine in memory-intensive applications, such as oceanographic research, that required the processing of enormous volumes of data. Although the VAX was not the first of what came to be called super-minicomputers, it soon became the standard by which those machines were measured, capturing 40 percent of the market.

The first version of UNIX for the VAX, however, made no provision for the computer's increased storage capacity. The Berkeley team fixed that oversight and also offered a faster-acting file system, enhanced text-editing software and a set of utilities for more efficient C programming. In addition, the Berkeley programmers adapted UNIX to a new kind of multi-user approach to computing known as distributed processing. The spread of minicomputers had created a rising demand for ways in which to link the machines, thereby combining their capabilities and allowing researchers to work simultaneously on different aspects of a single problem.

AT&T, which still owned UNIX, incorporated many of these features in subsequent versions of the software. By the mid-1980s, UNIX was arguably the most widely used operating system for midsized computers, licensed on more than 3,000 systems around the world. Like so many other advances in computing, it owed its success to grass-roots support from scientists, who recognized its ability to apply greater computing power to all aspects of their work, with less trouble than ever before.

Reconnaissance of the Microworld

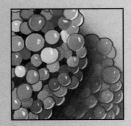

A fundamental tenet of biochemistry is that the structure of a molecule—the three-dimensional arrangement of its constituent atoms—determines how it works. Yet, scientists can directly observe neither the precise overall shapes of molecules nor their internal structures. Individual atoms are so small that waves of visible light pass by them as if they did not exist. Using an optical microscope to study the atoms in a molecule would be akin to fishing for minnows with a cargo net.

Obviously, a much finer net is needed to catch minnows, just as radiation of much shorter wavelength than visible light is needed for investigating the structure of molecules. X-rays meet this requirement, but they pose a technical problem: Unlike light, they are very difficult to focus into an image.

In the field of X-ray crystallography—the study of crystallized substances with X-ray "photography"—scientists sidestep this complication. From many different angles, they fire X-rays into a tiny crystal made of millions upon millions of identical molecules. The unusual photo session yields cryptic patterns of varying X-ray intensities. Working with these patterns in numerical form, a computer, using complex formulas that take advantage of the regularly repeating structure within a crystal, translates the patterns into an image of a single molecule.

Particularly intriguing to X-ray crystallographers are proteins, a large family of chemical compounds constructed from building blocks called amino acids—themselves groupings of as many as two dozen carbon, nitrogen, oxygen and hydrogen atoms. In cell membranes, proteins act as gatekeepers to admit nutrients and expel wastes; as enzymes, they control the pace of biochemical reactions; and as antibodies, they fight disease. The biological role of each protein rests on its shape, which determines its ability to interact with other molecules.

Proteins and other biological molecules such as DNA, which carries an organism's genetic code, begrudgingly surrender their structural details. Even with computers to handle the vast number of calculations required, scientists can labor years to unmask the positions of the atomic constituents. But the results are worth the effort. By exposing the relationship between structure and function, scientists uncover the molecular underpinnings of health and disease.

Difficult Structures to Know

By deciphering a protein's genetic code or by applying other methods, scientists can determine both the identity of the amino acids that make up the molecule and the sequence in which they are linked. While helpful, this information barely hints at the protein's intricate architecture—a bit like seeing an ornate sweater only as lengths of yarn.

In an average protein, hundreds of amino acids—each identified by an appendage called a side chain—are stitched together according to genetic instructions. The resulting strand of amino acids then spontaneously folds into a bundle of spirals and pleats that best reconciles the electrochemical forces present in the array. So immutable are the laws governing this behavior that a protein sequence consisting of upward of 10,000 atoms will always fold into exactly the same shape.

A chain of color-coded balls represents a small section of the amino acid sequence in a blood protein molecule. Amino acids take 20 common forms. As many as 1,000 of these building blocks may be combined to form a single protein.

The amino acid phenylalanine has an unusual side chain that includes an aromatic ring containing a distinctive circle of six carbon atoms (gray). Only three other amino acids have an aromatic ring, a fact that helps crystallographers determine the shape of a protein's molecule (pages 88-89).

In a crystal made of protein *(explained overleaf)*, the molecules—shown here as intricately folded bundles of amino acids—are regularly spaced and all oriented the same way. Between the protein molecules is a soup of various liquids necessary to moisten the crystal and keep it from disintegrating.

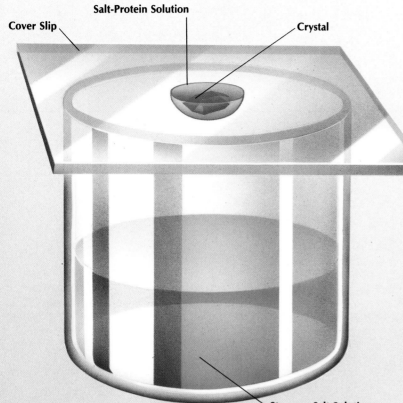

Cover Slip

Salt-Protein Solution

Crystal

Stronger Salt Solution

In one version of a crystal-making technique known as the vapor-diffusion method, a drop of a solution containing the salt ammonium sulfate and protein hangs from a cover slip above a stronger, protein-free salt solution. Water slowly evaporates from the drop at a rate influenced by the strength of the solution at the bottom of the tightly sealed container. As the drop loses water, protein molecules become more concentrated; some can no longer remain in solution. If the rate of evaporation and other factors are ideal, a suitable crystal may form within the drop.

An X-Ray View of a Crystal

It took researchers more than two decades to pin down the geometric organization of amino acids in hemoglobin, one of the first proteins to yield to crystallographic study. Advances in computers and technique have quickened the pace of discovery, but the procedure remains complex and uncertain of success.

It begins with mixing a variety of carefully chosen chemicals with a purified protein, then coaxing the molecules to organize themselves in a crystal, a degree of orderliness difficult to impose on these chemicals. Likened to prospecting for gold, making a crystal suitable for study draws heavily on the experience and intuition of practitioners and, on average, requires between two and four years of trial and error. Efforts to automate this labor-intensive step are under way, with some labs testing robotic systems.

During data collection, which ranks among the world's longer picture-taking sessions, a crystal is irradiated intermittently for hours—sometimes weeks—from many different angles. Upon striking the electrons in orbit around atomic nuclei within the protein molecules, the X-rays scatter in many directions. The intensity and the location of each X-ray is recorded on film or, as shown here, numerically registered by a computer-controlled device called an area detector (right). The result, known as an X-ray diffraction pattern, is the benchmark against which future estimates of the molecule's structure are compared.

X-Ray Source

Area Detector

Raw X-ray data appears as a bewildering array of spots displayed on a computer terminal from data collected by an area detector. Each spot (brighter ones indicate stronger X-rays) is a clue to the entire molecular structure of the protein.

Beam Stop

For each of many X-ray exposures, a protein crystal is precisely positioned by computer. An area detector measures X-rays scattered by the crystal (shown greatly enlarged here) and sends the resulting data to a computer. Between the crystal and the area detector, a lead beam-stop prevents the main X-ray beam from overwhelming the data-collection device.

Crystal

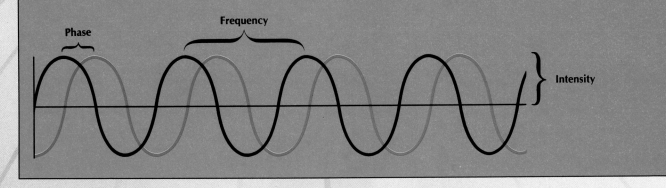

Profile of an X-Ray

Three properties of an X-ray—frequency, intensity and phase—must be known to read the information the X-ray contains about the structure of a protein molecule. Both of the rays drawn below have the same frequency, or number of wave crests passing a fixed point per second. They also have the same intensity, or amplitude, which is represented by the height of a wave crest. The waves differ, however, in phase—the position of a wave crest relative to a reference point, in this case the vertical line at the left of the diagram. In an X-ray crystallography diffraction pattern, the frequencies of all of the scattered X-rays are the same, equal to that of the original beam. An X-ray's intensity is gauged after it passes through the crystal, according to the digital output of a computerized area detector. Phase, which cannot be measured directly, must be inferred mathematically.

Phase

Frequency

Intensity

PHASE

INTENSITY

FREQUENCY

FOURIER

Recombining the Data

Having expressed X-rays captured by the area detector in terms of their basic components—intensity, frequency and phase—investigators can begin solving the molecule's structure. The computer does the bulk of the work through a mathematical process invented by 19th-century mathematician Jean Baptiste Fourier.

His complicated formulas work in two directions. In one, called Fourier analysis, the process can resolve the overtones of a complex sound wave or other periodic (regularly repeating) phenomena into their fundamental components. Working in reverse, the process is called Fourier synthesis. Applied in this manner, Fourier's equations can reassemble a whole from its many widely scattered pieces. X-rays diffracted by protein crystals lend themselves to the technique because a crystal is a periodic phenomenon—an arrangement of molecules repeated in three dimensions.

The drudgery of Fourier calculations is given to the computer, which produces series of digital contour maps *(represented graphically at right)* indicating the presence of atoms in the molecule as clusters of electrons that scattered the X-rays. Each map is an ultrathin slice of the protein molecule. The computer stacks the electron density maps and generates a rough outline of the protein *(far right)*, the first step toward an atom-by-atom rendering of the molecule *(page 89)*.

Phase, intensity and frequency for each detected X-ray are fed into a computer that is programmed to perform Fourier synthesis. The computer's solution yields the density of electrons at a given site in a single protein molecule.

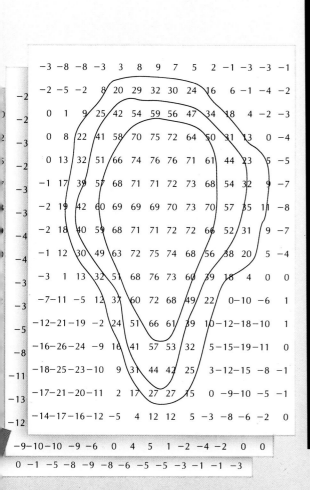

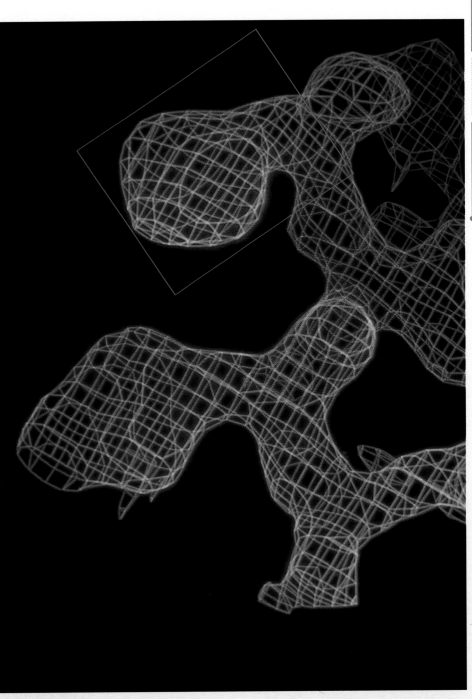

Slices of a molecule consist of number arrays representing concentrations of electrons. Lines connecting numbers of similar or equal values form contours that can be read as a topographical map. The smallest, closed shape reveals a peak of electron density; progressively larger outlines link points of diminishing density. The map above charts the clustering of electrons in the aromatic ring in the side chain of phenylalanine, shown on page 82, and the carbon atom that joins it to the rest of the amino acid.

Numbers resulting from Fourier synthesis are assembled by computer into a three-dimensional view of the protein's electron-density contours. Only a small portion of the whole is reproduced here, with a red box superimposed to show the position of the aromatic ring outlined in the contour map at left. The initial version of the electron concentrations is cruder than this one, which has already been partially refined by the process described on the next two pages.

Refining the Structure

Having produced a pattern of electrons like the one shown on page 87, the crystallographer must next determine how the protein's string of amino acids fits into this assembly of electron clouds. The fitting process relies on the computer's ability to display and reorient three-dimensional shapes on its screen. Watching the display, the crystallographer manipulates a variety of computer controls to superimpose amino acids on the model of the protein *(left)*. Since the image is imprecise at this stage, the initial fitting yields only an approximation of the actual structure.

For a more precise rendition of the molecule, the crystallographer refines the structure, using a cyclical process *(below)* in which the theoretical structure obtained from a fitting is compared with the X-ray diffraction data obtained from the real protein. The comparison, involving numerous geometrical and statistical computations, suggests to the crystallographer improvements that might bring the trial structure closer to the original.

Several refinement cycles are necessary to achieve an accurate picture of a protein *(right)*. Success, usually the result of painstaking efforts lasting many weeks, pays off in a variety of medical and scientific gains *(pages 90-91)*.

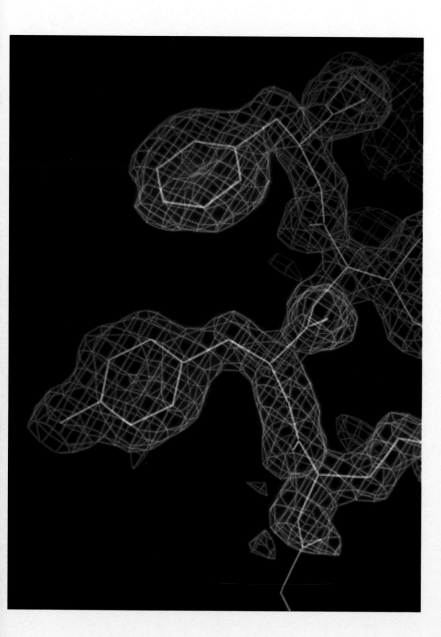

Red hexagons mark clusters of electrons that suggest the presence of amino acid side chains having aromatic rings. This observation narrows the possible identities of the amino acids. A crystallographer added the hexagons based on this observation and on the known sequence of amino acids in the molecule. Additional red lines are positioned where the researcher believes parts of other amino acids fit into the outline, shown here after several applications of the process outlined at right.

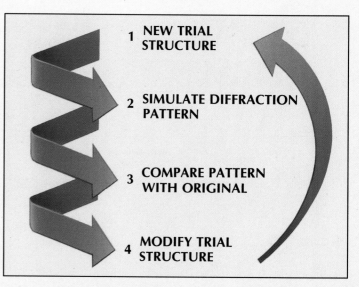

1 **NEW TRIAL STRUCTURE**

2 **SIMULATE DIFFRACTION PATTERN**

3 **COMPARE PATTERN WITH ORIGINAL**

4 **MODIFY TRIAL STRUCTURE**

Refinement begins with an estimate of amino acid positions in the protein. An X-ray pattern for the trial structure is generated and compared by computer with the actual protein's pattern. To narrow differences, the trial structure is altered, and the cycle begins anew.

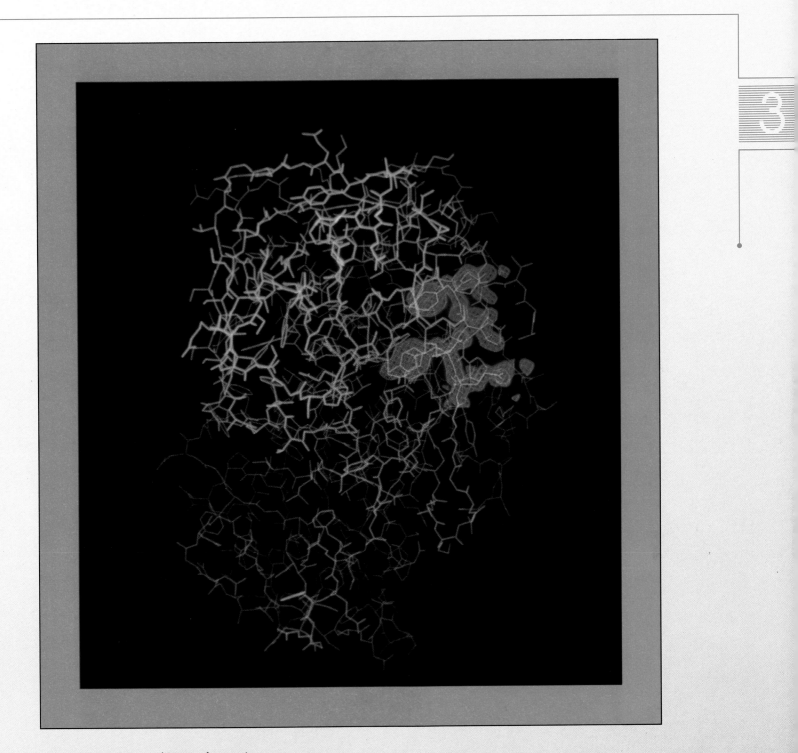

This computer-generated image of a protein
molecule's structure highlights the positions of
the amino acid side chains that appear on
the opposite page, as well as the complex
folding of amino acids and the bonds,
represented by sticklike projections, between
atoms. Some amino acids lie deep inside the
globular protein, and others sit on the surface,
poised to interact with other molecules.

89

The Chemistry of Life

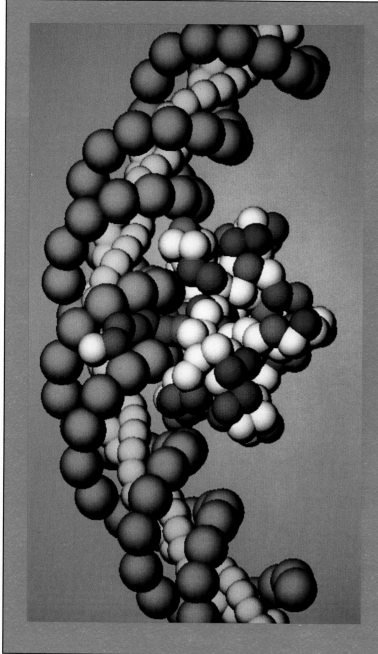

A viral protein called the cro repressor
attaches to a molecule of the organism's DNA
in this computer image—derived, like the
other images on these pages, from the work
of X-ray crystallographers. The protein fits
snugly into a helical groove of the DNA
molecule, permitting the virus to multiply.

White balls representing the protein troponin
nestle alongside blue spheres of actin
and a diagonally positioned molecule of
tropomyosin. When stimulated by calcium
atoms, the three proteins constitute
a fast-acting trigger for a muscle fiber.

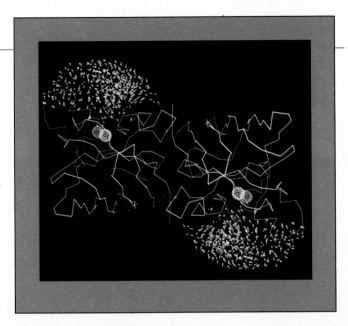

Amino acids *(zigzag lines)* in the enzyme superoxide dismutase are arranged in such a way that electrical forces are created *(arrows)*. They attract toxic, negatively charged by-products of oxygen consumption (not shown) toward positively charged ions of copper *(blue spheres)* and zinc *(pink spheres)*, where the copper neutralizes harmful substances.

Antibodies, foot soldiers in the battle against disease, latch onto a plant virus 10 times their size as a prelude to its destruction. Knowing the arrangement of amino acids that makes such attachments possible assists researchers in their efforts to create vaccines.

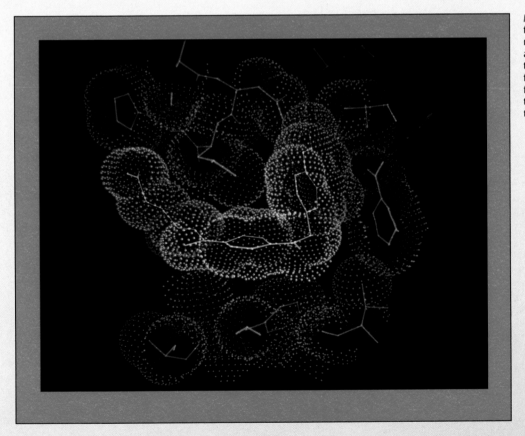

Mimicking the shape of the vitamin folic acid, an anticancer drug called methotrexate *(red spheres)* links with an enzyme *(blue spheres)* that converts the vitamin into compounds essential for making DNA. By substituting itself for the vitamin, methotrexate disrupts the conversion process, depriving tumor cells of the means to reproduce.

92

Revelations Unlimited

Contrary to popular belief, a raindrop in its short life never assumes the shape of a teardrop. Since the turn of the century, scientists have known that raindrops assume a flattened shape, somewhat like that of a hamburger bun. Now, from laboratory experiments and computer modeling, scientists have learned that, as raindrops fall, they stretch and swell, thin and bulge in a way determined by such factors as their size and the surrounding air pressure. High-speed movies of raindrops taken under controlled conditions in wind tunnels have confirmed this behavior, and scientists have traced the origin of the oscillations to collisions between large raindrops as they overtake and run into smaller ones.

Raindrop oscillations account for the broken, streaked appearance of rain when illuminated by a car's headlights. In effect, each drop acts as a variable lens that refracts or bends the headlight beam in different directions as the raindrop changes shape. The rain is seen as a streak so long as the raindrop refracts the beam in the observer's direction; but as the raindrop changes shape, it refracts the beam away from the observer and the streak vanishes.

Why falling drops of water appear as they do in the headlights of an automobile on a dark and stormy night would seem to rank among the most useless bits of scientific arcana, right alongside the number of acacia-tree seed pods an African nomad's goat eats. But these facts and others, such as those learned from detailed measurements of the world's ocean surfaces or attempts to maintain gases at a temperature hotter than the interior of the sun, contribute much to humankind's awareness of the world, how people live in it today and how they might prosper tomorrow.

Though ostensibly unrelated, these avenues of scientific inquiry share a common bond: Without computers, they would all probably be dead ends. Controlling hot gases—plasma, in the language of the physicists who study the subject—requires coordinating so many devices, so rapidly and so precisely that experiments in the field of plasma physics would be unthinkable without computers to manage them. Surveying millions of square miles of sea surface or collating hundreds of influences on an African society's way of life would be fools' errands without computers to make sense of the mountains of data that such studies amass. And the implications of the fact that raindrops change shape as they descend to earth might still be unappreciated.

THE MICROWAVE CONNECTION
The practical consequences of raindrop dynamics relate to the water globules' ability to scatter microwaves—radio signals similar to light but lower in frequency. Communications companies such as telephone and telegraph services use microwaves to transmit conversations where laying wires is impractical because of inhospitable terrain or landowners who refuse access to their property. Telephone signals carried on microwaves are electronically separated into dis-

93

crete frequency bands so that conversations do not interfere with one another. But oscillating raindrops can reduce the separation between bands. When that occurs, a long-distance telephone conversation, for example, can be overheard, however faintly, by participants in another.

Better understanding of raindrop behavior cannot only improve the quality and reliability of communications, it can also contribute to better weather prediction. Radar, a tool as essential to modern meteorology as the barometer, bounces microwaves off the water droplets in storms. Meteorologists try to gauge from the image of a storm on a radar scope its position, intensity, and also the size of its raindrops—and thereby to predict how much rain can be expected along the storm's path. But only by understanding the complex relationship between the size of a drop and the way its oscillation pattern scatters microwaves can scientists arrive at accurate estimates of raindrop size and the volume of precipitation that might be expected.

LINKING RAINDROPS AND MICROWAVES
In the 1970s, when this scattering effect was no more than a theory, Kenneth V. Beard, a doctoral student in meteorology at the University of California at Los Angeles, decided to undertake an investigation of raindrop behavior. The task of doing so, he realized, would be greatly eased if he could enlist the aid of computers to perform the voluminous analysis and comparison of experimental results with theoretical predictions.

Beard's experimental work was based on the observation of droplets of water as they fell in vertical wind tunnels, which simulate the wind resistance encountered by raindrops as they accelerate to maximum velocity. He began by developing mathematical expressions that would describe the way the drops changed shape—as well as the speeds at which they fell, the rates at which they evaporated on the way to earth and the growth of raindrops through collisions. "It was relatively simple stuff—all algebra and calculus," he later recalled. But the calculations made up in bulk what they lacked in complexity, and a computer proved indispensable. Beard wrote his early programs in FORTRAN, a computer language frequently used for scientific purposes, and fed them into UCLA's IBM mainframe with punched cards. For simple calculations while developing his raindrop model, he relied on a programmable calculator.

After moving to the University of Illinois in 1974, Beard transferred most of his programs to a Cyber 175, a powerful computer made by Control Data Corporation. The Illinois machine was equipped with an arsenal of peripherals, including equipment for converting masses of numbers into crude images of raindrops. These renderings, which resembled chicken wire in their structure, let a viewer see through the object from front to rear. Economical with computer memory, such so-called wireframe images suited Beard and others deeply immersed in the study of raindrops, but they were potentially confusing to nonexperts. So in the early 1980s, Beard set to work on his own image-producing software, incorporating algorithms capable of generating a spectacular sequence of shaded, three-dimensional raindrop images like the ones reproduced on pages 96 and 97.

The impetus for embarking on the substantial task of writing these programs was a symposium of European communications engineers that Beard was to address on the subject of measuring rainfall by radar. "I wanted to communicate with the radar experts, who weren't familiar with raindrop theory," he recalled. "The reaction at the symposium was unbelievable. People really sat up and took notice. They could understand the drop shapes and the oscillation modes, and I could tell them the scientific story as I went through the images with them."

In addition to communicating his ideas, Beard has found computer graphics valuable in refining his theories about raindrop dynamics. "We've been able to generate computer images of what oscillations might look like, then compare these theoretical photographs with actual photographs of raindrops taken in a wind tunnel." To create the drops that are sent plunging down the wind tunnel, Beard uses a jet of water controlled by a desktop computer, which not only breaks the stream into droplets of uniform size and initial velocity, but handles the photographic aspects of the experiment by triggering strobe lights and cameras at just the right instants. The laboratory drops—mathematical and real— match up so well that scientists can feel confident in using the model to seek benefits in the fast-expanding realm of microwave technology.

THE RAIN IN KENYA

Beard's focus on the shapes of raindrops would seem bizarre to the nomadic herders of the vast East African savanna. Following a way of life unchanged for centuries, these stoic people are concerned only that enough rain comes to them, never mind whether the drops are long and thin or short and squat. An endless cycle of wet and dry seasons keeps tribal groups, such as the Turkana of northwest Kenya, constantly on the move through their arid Rift Valley home land in search of forage for their mixed herds of cattle, camels, sheep, goats and donkeys. Their eyes are their weather radar, reading deluge or drought in the look of the sky.

The sparse grass, shrubs and acacia trees of the savanna have an austere beauty, but living there has never been easy. Although annual rainfall averages more than 10 inches a year—about the amount that the drier regions of the American Great Plains receive—most of it comes during a brief wet season that begins in March and lasts into May. Even in the best of years, the average adult subsists on about 1,300 calories a day, about half the energy intake of a typical American. When one Turkana hails another with the greeting "Any news?" a likely response is "No—I'm only hungry." This saying notwithstanding, conditions may seem worse than they actually are. The Turkana pursue an active life, but it is virtually devoid of heavy labor; even women are assisted by beasts of burden. Thus, these nomads probably need less food than they would require if they were farmers.

Social scientists have long assumed that subsistence problems are inherent in the life of pastoral nomads, whose lands are used in common by all members of the group. Experts have argued that pastoralism leads herders to raise perhaps twice as many animals as they need for food in order to ensure the survival of the nucleus for a new herd in the event of consecutive years of drought. Common use of the land provides no incentive to graze an area lightly and move on; what one family's herd leaves behind, the next family's will devour. Inevitably, the animals overgraze the range and gradually destroy it. Often, the solution

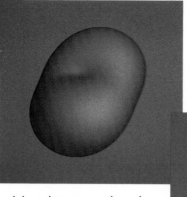

advocated has been to abandon pastoralism in favor of farming or ranching, in which exclusive use of the land rewards those who do not devastate it.

Beginning in 1980, scientists at Colorado State University's Natural Resource Ecology Laboratory undertook a novel investigation of the Turkana and their environment. The ecologists and their colleagues in other fields proposed to subject the Turkana to a detailed energy-flow analysis, in which the tribespeople would be viewed as consumers of solar energy stored in the plants that their herds converted to milk and meat. The concept of energy flow applies equally to pastoralism, farming and ranching, providing a common ruler by which to measure the merits of each in the harsh climate of East Africa.

The first challenge faced by the researchers was to use a computer to build a detailed simulation model of the Turkana way of life. Such a model represents important elements of a system by assigning numeric values to them; by manipulating the numbers, a scientist can see the effects caused by changes in different elements. The Turkana model tracked the flow of energy from plants through animals, both wild and domesticated, to people. The model even included representations of actual biological processes such as photosynthesis, protein production and metabolism in order to estimate energy losses that occur at each step in the food chain crowned by the nomads.

In creating the model, ecologists David M. Swift and Michael B. Coughenour of the Colorado State team, along with their colleagues, first identified environmental factors that affected the amount of food available to Turkana herds. Among the most important were ambient temperature, daily rainfall, soil moisture levels and the digestibility of various types of forage at different times of the year. The researchers also worked into the model how much goats, cattle, sheep and camels ate of each plant type, as well as the response of the Turkana to the effects of drought on their herds. Much of the Turkana's nourishment comes from milk: In hard times, the herders may get three quarters of their calories from this source. If milk production declines because the animals are hungry, the herders have several choices: They can bleed an animal, consuming the protein-rich liquid to augment the diminished supply of milk. They can slaughter the animal, or they can barter it for corn. If an animal is too emaciated to be bled, the Turkana would rather trade it than kill it, but if forced to sacrifice part of a herd, they prefer killing goats to camels, in part because the meat from smaller animals can be consumed more quickly, reducing the possibility of spoiling in the African heat.

Woven from hundreds of such constants and variables, the model's algorithms faithfully represented the complex relationships within the Turkana ecosystem. Equations encompassing temperature, rainfall and sunlight determined the photosynthesis rates of dwarf shrubs, grasses and other vegetation on which the Turkana herds depend. Other mathematical statements described the herds' gain or loss of weight under varying climatic conditions. And finally, the model linked these equations so that the results from one influenced the solution of another. "Most people," said Swift, "can't work out the relationships of more than two or three variables in their heads, but the computer's capacity is limitless."

Creating such a model compels the builders to think about an ecosystem more deeply—and to examine its interrelationships with greater care—than they might do otherwise. "Each step in putting together a model," observed Swift, "represents a hypothesis about how something in the system works. The first time you run a simulation, the results never look very much like the real world. Finding the wrong hypothesis and correcting it leads to a new and more accurate version of the model to replace the previous one."

DESCRIBING DIET BY COUNTING BITES

The feat of describing the Turkana lifestyle to the computers, though intellectually challenging, seems but a parlor game compared with the physical difficulties of gathering the information required by the model to perform its analysis. Most of the data for the model came from laborious field surveys. Beginning in April 1981, groups of scientists accompanied families and their herds as they wandered the savanna. Every day, researchers observed individual animals as they foraged, recording their diet in exhaustive detail. The data was quantified by the bite-count method. Each time a browsing animal took a nibble, the onlooking scientist tallied it. Equipped with a hand-held tape recorder, the observer also noted the type of plant and the part of it that the animal selected. During one phase of the study, researchers recorded approximately 350,000 bites in this manner.

Ground observations and aerial surveys determined the distribution and diversity of plants in different vegetation zones. The total number of acacia-tree seed pods—a favorite forage for goats and sheep in the wet season—was estimated by counting the acacias in an area and multiplying that number by the pod production for a typical tree. To account for noneating ways in which the Turkana consumed solar energy that was stored in plants, investigators weighed the

The dimple in this computer-generated raindrop, captured in simulated free fall to earth, occurs after collisions with other raindrops cause the drop to pulsate. By studying the shape from many viewpoints, as shown here, researchers can better correlate the oscillations of raindrops with their scattering effect on the beams of weather radar in order to arrive at more accurate forecasts.

firewood collected by four families and extrapolated to a figure for the entire tribe. The meddlesome observers even disassembled huts and corrals and weighed the component sticks to assess the quantity of wood that was used for construction.

Having assembled their mountain of data, the scientists used the computer model as a crystal ball to see what might befall the Turkana under various circumstances. For example, the algorithms could predict changes in the size and composition of Turkana herds if the savanna suffered two successive years of drought, or three years or four, and how this hardship might affect the growth rate of Turkana children.

Contrary to the results of earlier studies, the computer model strongly suggested that the Turkana live in reasonable harmony with their environment. Ecologists believe that stability in an ecosystem increases with the flexibility of the food chain: The greater the number of pathways for energy to find its way from plants to humans, the more resilient the ecosystem appears to be. The Colorado State model traced more than 30 such pathways among the Turkana, suggesting a food web—rather than a food chain—that helps the nomads survive difficult times by moving their herds and adjusting their diets as environmental conditions change.

Close observation of the Turkana seems to confirm the model's conclusions. When Swift's group first began to study the tribe in 1980, the region was just recovering from a serious drought. "In nearby regions outside the study area," Swift recalled, "there were famine-relief camps set up. The pathways of energy flow there were less flexible, and in some cases families had lost 50 to 90 percent of their herds. In the study area, however, livestock losses were severe but tolerable. Even without relief camps, there were no reports of people starving to death. When we did our initial health surveys we found a lot of the men carrying the same percentage of body fat as world-class marathoners. They were lean, and would have been happy to have more food, but they weren't ill."

SLOPES OF THE BOUNDING MAIN

The Turkana and sharp-eyed meteorologists at the consoles of their weather radars would agree, from their different points of view, that water is one of the earth's miracles. New rain is ancient moisture, recycled in a never-ending process of evaporation and precipitation. What falls from the clouds on the Turkana and the rest of the world's inhabitants fills streams that swell lakes. They in turn feed rivers that roll to the sea, earth's grand depository for this life-giving fluid.

Until recently, the surface of the ocean was thought, if not to be flat, at least to be level, the heights of its crests compensated by the depths of its troughs. Sea level, after all, is the universal benchmark with which the height of many an object or structure is compared. But as geophysicists came to understand the effect of gravity upon the ocean, they realized that sea level would be higher where the earth's irregular gravitational field was strong and lower where it was weak. This concept remained purely theoretical, however, in the absence of instruments to measure the undulation. Not until 1969, as a result of a conference of earth scientists at Williams College in Massachusetts, was there serious discussion of trying to chart the surface of the oceans.

Out of this gathering came the idea for placing a superaccurate radar altimeter aboard a satellite in earth orbit. The altimeter would measure the height of the sea below it by noting the time required by radar pulses transmitted from space to reach earth and return. Differences of a few milliseconds in recorded times would be translated into an extraordinarily detailed topographical map showing the height of all the oceans on the earth.

A prototype altimeter went aloft aboard the Skylab manned observatory in 1973. At the times scheduled for work on the experiment, the Skylab astronauts rolled their spacecraft to point the altimeter's dish antenna straight down. To avoid disturbing the antenna and generating erroneous readings, all other activity aboard the satellite ceased. When the measurements were later analyzed and converted to contour maps, they proved that the idea of radar altimetry was a sound one for measuring ocean topography. They indicated, for example, the existence of "bumps" in the surface as high as 26 feet around the Cape Verde Islands seamounts off the West Coast of Africa.

James G. Marsh, a NASA geophysicist who has played a key role in the development of satellite altimetry, recalls taking the Skylab data to a conference of earth scientists the following year. "The classical geophysicists were incredulous," Marsh remembers. "In their eyes it just couldn't be true—the instruments must have been providing false readings. It took a couple of years to win the acceptance of the geophysical community. But we knew the data were of good quality."

Close examination showed that the "surface variations we found matched well with the known shape of the ocean floor." Up to this time, oceanographers' knowledge of the sea bottom depended on sonar soundings from surface ships, a laborious method that left much of the ocean floor—especially in the remote seas near Antarctica—incompletely charted. Now it appeared that radar altimetry might enable scientists to trace in greater detail than ever before the awesome trenches and towering ridges beneath the waves.

A SATELLITE FOR SEA DUTY

Mapping the ocean surface by radar altimetry came into its own with a three-ton satellite launched by NASA in the summer of 1978. Known as Seasat, it circled the planet 14 times a day in a criss-cross pattern over all but the polar regions. Seasat carried an altimeter capable of discerning differences in the height of the sea as small as two inches. In addition, a battery of sensors collected information about many other sea conditions, including winds, temperatures, wave heights and direction, currents and tides, and the amount of water in the atmosphere above the ocean. Although a massive short circuit silenced the satellite after just three months in orbit, Seasat provided scientists with more data on the world's oceans than had been collected during the previous century. In all, the satellite's altimeter operated for more than 1,500 hours. Transmitting radar pulses at the rate of one each second, Seasat provided some 5.5 million measurements of the ocean's height.

Seasat's radar eye owed its acuity to a computerized system that accurately measured the time it took for radar signals to flash to the ocean and back—about one ten-billionth of a second. Such information would be of little use without

The Ocean's Rumpled Surface

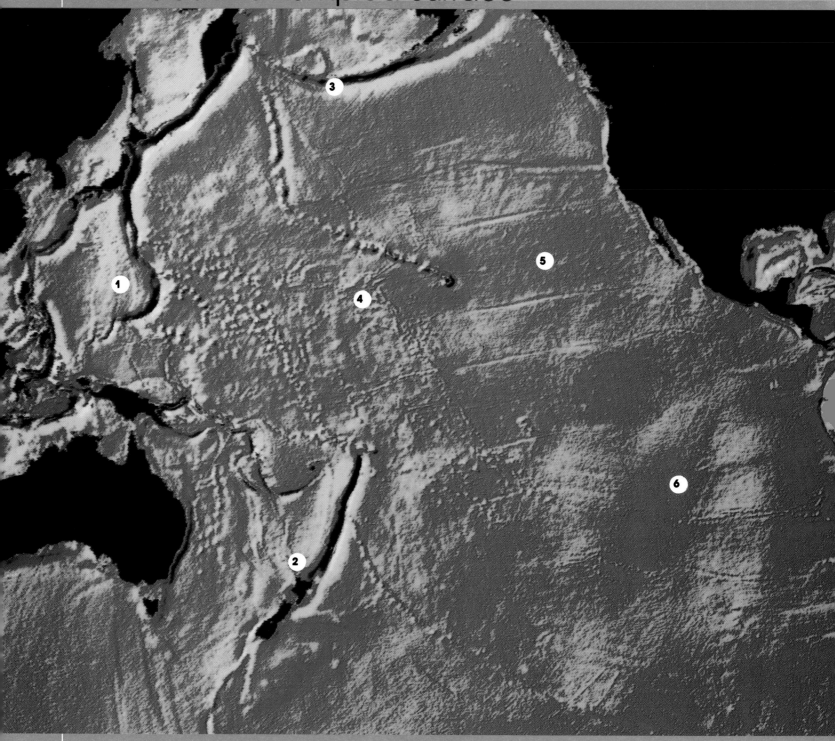

This computer-enhanced image, produced from radar-altimetry data gathered by satellite and refined by computers on earth, reveals that the surface of the world's oceans has a topography echoing features of the sea floor. Variations in the earth's gravitational field around submarine mountains and canyons produce the watery hills and valleys, which may rise or dip as much as 100 feet. Some of the surface features in the western Pacific correspond to deep ocean-floor gashes: the Marianas Trench (1), the Tonga Trench (2) and the Aleutian Trench (3). Small, tightly clustered bumps (4) are related to islands and

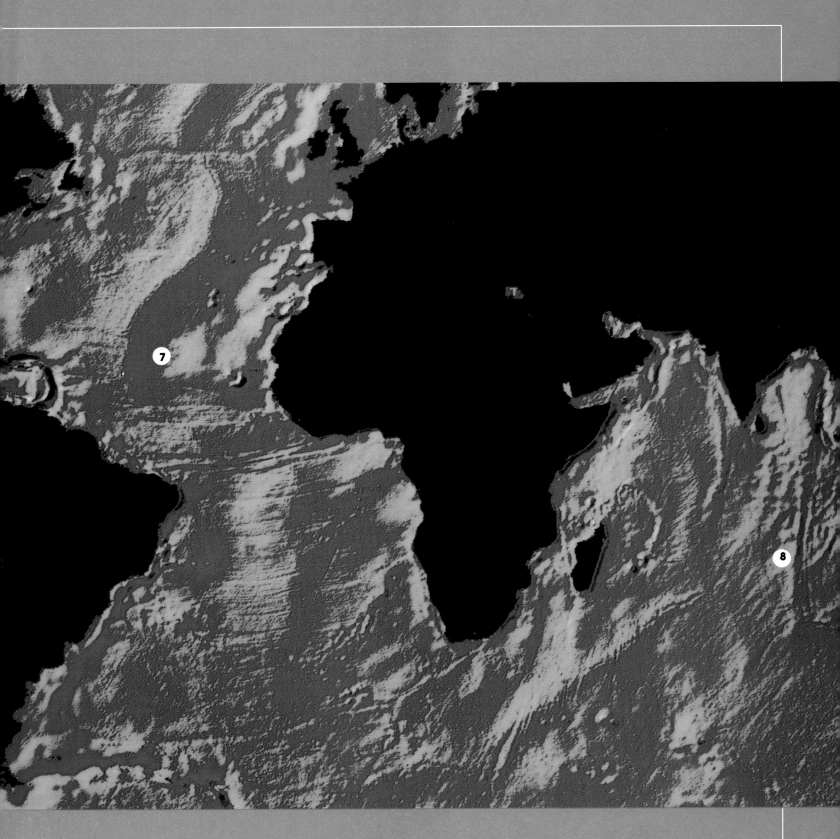

submerged mountains called seamounts, while horizontal slashes in the eastern Pacific (5) are surface effects of stress fractures in one of the gigantic plates of rock that form the earth's crust. Large, rounded bulges (6) may indicate where upwellings of molten material within the earth's crust—thought to be the driving force behind plate movement—have heated the overlying water, causing it to pile up in low mounds. Between North America and Africa are the surface manifestations of the Mid-Atlantic Ridge (7), and running north and south in the Indian Ocean is watery echo of the Ninety-East Ridge (8), named for its longitude.

an accurate determination of the satellite's altitude. It is no simple task to estimate—with the accuracy required for radar altimetry of the sea surface—how high a satellite is flying. Doing so required the mathematical ingenuity of more than a dozen scientists—and the crucial assistance of a laser range finder located in Bermuda.

Another digital timer, precise to 10 millionths of a second, helped determine Seasat's exact orbital position, so that data could later be correlated with points on the sea surface. The information from the altimeter and other sensors was stored on magnetic tapes until the satellite came within radio range of a NASA telemetry station. These facilities, scattered around the world, relayed the data to a preprocessing station at White Sands, New Mexico, where it was converted to a form that would be useful in subsequent analysis. Then the Jet Propulsion Laboratory (JPL) near Los Angeles went to work on the altimeter data, compensating for the rise and fall of ocean tides, the irrelevant disturbances of ocean waves, and the varying effects of the atmosphere on the radar signals.

After processing, the information was stored in a database at JPL. Scientists at government labs, in industry and at universities, were all linked through a nationwide communications network to the computer that managed the database; they could sift through the information for revelations about the effect of ocean currents on weather, about the location of offshore oil deposits or about the huge, floating masses, or plates, that make up the earth's crust. Of all the data gathered, none was more intriguing than the figures describing the ocean's surface topography. They proved that the sea surface echoes features of the ocean floor. "The ocean surface is like a blanket thrown over all that rugged terrain," says Marsh.

Where undersea mountains increase the strength of the gravitational field, ocean water is pulled into gentle rises; troughs appear over trenches, where the field is weaker. Moreover, the sea surface is higher above warm water than it is where the ocean is cold. The Gulf Stream and the other great currents of the world's oceans turn out to be the result of water running down subtle declines, hundreds or thousands of miles long but no more than five feet high. The speed of a current, calculated from the angle of the slope, agrees almost exactly with the progress of buoys set adrift to measure the stream's velocity.

Among those most interested in Seasat's altimetry were geophysicists at NASA's Goddard Space Flight Center in Greenbelt, Maryland. Using a Cyber 205 supercomputer and a smaller VAX 11/780 computer, the scientists converted the data into striking contour maps of the seas by means of special computer-graphics techniques. The final step in the imaging process, known as edge enhancement, simulates the shadows cast by light from a single source. Typically, this technique is used to illuminate the scene from the northwest, so that ridges on the ocean, for example, appear to be highlighted on the western flank and to cast a shadow to the east (pages 100-101).

KEEPING UP WITH THE DATA

In a field such as radar altimetry, the development of computer techniques for structuring the masses of experimental information into a meaningful form may run years behind the technology used to gather and analyze it. Nearly a decade after Seasat fell silent, scientists had not yet exhausted the riches it provided. "We've made great progress in the use of computers to analyze massive amounts of data," observes Marsh, "but we have much further to go." Ideas for the future include computer programs and special computer-graphics workstations that will allow a researcher sitting at a console with a joystick, often used in playing computer games, to move quickly to any spot on the world's oceans, to zoom in for a close-up or back away for a longer view.

Scientists anticipate even greater data-handling challenges from TOPEX (The Ocean Topography Experiment), an American-French satellite scheduled for launch in 1992. TOPEX is intended to study ocean currents with the expectation of learning how they influence the earth's weather on a global scale. Currents in the southern Pacific Ocean, for example, are known to play a key role in El Niño, a high-pressure weather system that appears at intervals of two to 10 years off the coast of Peru. When it occurs, trade winds diminish and allow warm surface currents to push toward the coast. There they smother the normal upwelling of cool, plankton-rich water, often with calamitous effects on sea life and weather patterns. But precisely how El Niño, in its waxings and wanings, triggers drought thousands of miles away in North America remains to be explained.

TOPEX will orbit more than 800 miles above the earth, yet it will be able to record ocean heights to an accuracy of less than an inch. Moreover, TOPEX's experiments will be coordinated with simultaneous data-collection activities of other satellites, aircraft, ships and radio-beacon buoys dropped into the ocean to help determine the speed and direction of currents.

Inventing ways for computers to winnow this abundance—at least double the amount of information recorded by Seasat—presents a great challenge to the investigators. Marsh, for one, is optimistic: He expects that scientists will create programs capable of reliable forecasting months into the future. "The best we can do now," he says, "is to make 'hindcasts' by showing, for instance, how El Niño affected ocean temperature, which in turn affected rainfall in Peru or other parts of the Western Hemisphere. But given the complexity of global weather systems, this itself is an accomplishment."

HARNESSING THE POWER OF THE STARS

Marsh may view the sea with renewed interest because of its unexpected tendency to pile up on itself, but other scientists see the broad expanse of the world's oceans as a limitless source of energy, not through the motion of its waves or the power of the weather it spawns, but because of one of its elements. The waters of the earth contain more than 10 trillion tons of deuterium, an isotope of hydrogen with an extra neutron in its nucleus. Easily separated from water, deuterium has the potential to be the main fuel for an energy-producing reaction called nuclear fusion—if only the problems of controlling that reaction can be overcome. In outline, controlled fusion seems straightforward: Deuterium is combined with a lesser amount of tritium (another hydrogen isotope with two extra neutrons) and subjected to intense heat in a near-vacuum. Under these conditions, the forces that cause the particles in the nuclei of the isotopes to repel each other can be overcome. Colliding, they can recombine to produce helium nuclei; the by-products are additional heat and fast-moving neutrons. The heat can help sustain the reaction, but the neutrons escape. In a fusion-fired power plant, the neutrons would crash into a "blanket" of material that converts the energy of the collisions into heat; this heat would be tapped to make steam, and the steam, in turn, would drive dynamos that generate electricity.

Nuclear fusion is the process that heats the sun and generates the destructive power of the hydrogen bomb. For three decades, scientists have dreamed of harnessing it, knowing that the energy needs of humankind would be satisfied for millennia. Not only would fuel be plentiful, but fusion—unlike fission reactors—produces short-lived, relatively harmless radioactive debris. (Most of the longer-lasting radiation from a hydrogen bomb comes from its trigger, a uranium fission bomb that creates the heat required for fusion.) Mastery of nuclear fusion has been called technology's holy grail. But after a generation of pursuit, physicists have only managed to narrow the gap separating them from their goal. Skeptics believe the technological difficulties may never be surmounted. Even the most optimistic scientists do not expect to see construction of a commercial fusion-reactor power plant before the year 2020.

A TECHNOLOGICAL ALP

One of the most advanced facilities for research on controlled nuclear fusion is the Princeton Plasma Physics Laboratory (PPPL), a sprawling complex that is located in central New Jersey about three miles from Princeton University's main campus. It traces its roots to a scientific inspiration that occurred in 1951—incongruously, not in a laboratory but on a ski lift in Colorado. Riding the lift was Lyman Spitzer Jr., a vacationing astrophysicist from Princeton. Spitzer was pondering recent newspaper accounts of an Argentine scientist who had supposedly found a way of unlocking the fusion genie. Although the reports turned out to be false (Argentine dictator Juan Peron, having first awarded the scientist a medal, later had him jailed), they set Spitzer thinking about how a fusion reaction might be contained. He persuaded the U.S. government to fund a modest research program. An enthusiastic mountaineer as well as skier, Spitzer dubbed the program Project Matterhorn as a measure of the challenge that lay ahead.

The problem lies in containing the hydrogen isotopes at the necessary 100 million degrees Celsius—about six times as hot as the sun's interior. At this temperature the fuel becomes a plasma—a state of matter where all nuclei are separated from their electrons and move freely through space. If the particles can be confined long enough—a fraction of a second is sufficient—collisions between bare nuclei will result in fusion. But keeping the plasma together is not easy. It cannot be physically constrained by a walled chamber; in merely touching a wall, the particles would cool below the temperature necessary to sustain the reaction.

Generating and sustaining a plasma has been likened to holding together jelly with rubber bands. For Project Matterhorn, Spitzer settled on a technique of magnetic confinement, to be achieved with a device called the stellarator. A closed tube shaped like a race track, the stellarator was surrounded by an array of electrical coils that generated strong magnetic fields shaped so that charged plasma particles would always be deflected toward the center of the tube. During the 1950s, a series of stellarators was built at Princeton, increasing in size and complexity. In the 1960s, researchers at what had now become the PPPL turned their attention to the tokamak, an apparatus similar in principle to the stellarator. This doughnut-shaped device, conceived in the early 1950s by scientists in the Soviet Union, was named with the Russian acronym for "toroidal magnetic container." In 1982, PPPL unveiled its largest version of the Soviet invention—the Tokamak Fusion Test Reactor, or TFTR. The 1,500-ton behemoth was designed to be the first fusion reactor to reach the break-even point, where the energy produced would be at least as great as the energy required to trigger the reaction—about 30 megawatts. Princeton scientists hope to achieve that goal in the early 1990s.

The $314 million TFTR stands nearly four stories high, its core obscured by an immense superstructure of girders, pipes and electronic cables. Entwined in this high-tech complex is a network of fiber optics linking the TFTR to the computers that function as its central nervous system. The computer system includes a control center equipped with 12 Gould/SEL minicomputers to coordinate the thousands of digital activities involved in regulating each fusion experiment and in monitoring and recording the results. An auxiliary system built around a cluster of VAX computers helps researchers analyze data and provides communication via satellite with Cray supercomputers, used for simulating plasma flow, at Lawrence Livermore National Laboratory in California.

PULSES OF POWER

A typical TFTR experiment takes only a few minutes, with the fusion reaction itself happening in a fraction of a second. Each pulse, as the reactions are called, is designed to explore the characteristics of a plasma under a very specific set of conditions, in order to help determine the density, temperature and shape required for successful fusion. Because the hot particles are always shifting within the tokamak, the TFTR computer system must monitor the plasma continuously and adjust the reactor's systems to keep it confined. To do so, the computers handle information from an array of more than 17,000 sensors that measure such attributes as the electrical currents in the coils and in the plasma, and the temperature, density and X-ray radiation of the plasma. The computers process this data immediately, then send instructions to the 7,000-odd control modules that can adjust such variables as the power being delivered to the coils or the intensity of the particle beam—an accelerated stream of deuterium—used to heat the plasma.

Preparation for an experiment begins in a room lined with color consoles displaying the status of TFTR systems, where a team of 50 or more physicists and engineers carefully feeds the computer system information that it will use to program the control modules. Two minutes before the reaction is to begin, the physicist in charge presses a red START button. This action turns the experiment over to the TFTR computers, which encode the scientists' instructions into the thousands of specific and meticulously coordinated actions necessary for the TFTR to create the plasma. A countdown begins, with the operation of the tokamak's components following a precise sequence synchronized by an electronic clock ticking a million times a second. The computer system begins monitoring the plasma, taking "snapshots" of the readings from all system sensors every two seconds. A snapshot two tenths of a second before the pulse is to begin provides a final chance to abort the experiment and start the countdown over. If conditions in the tokamak are correct, however, the computers switch on the power that initiates the fusion pulse. When the pulse ends, the computers terminate the experiment by turning off the power and begin the task of sifting through the data for meaningful results. Performing six million operations per second, the TFTR computer system collects in excess of 40 million bytes of data—equivalent to more than 14,000 pages of *The Encyclopaedia Britannica*—for every pulse. In seven and a half minutes, the system is ready to do another pulse.

The Princeton research involves a division of labor among physicists. Some of them specialize in making predictions about how the plasma should behave given a certain set of conditions. Others test those predictions, and the results of their investigations suggest new theories about the plasma churning within the reactor vessel. Ned R. Sauthoff, the physicist who headed PPPL's computer division in the mid-1980s, noted that there is nothing tidy about plasma: "It wrinkles, twists and spins. Experimentalists measure these deformities and other anomalies, while the theorists try to figure out what instabilities or other factors might give rise to them. The two groups have a lively discourse as to whether or not the theories are right. That's where the real physics gets done."

The colloquy among Princeton's plasma physicists is typical of the process behind advances in every area of modern science—and so is the critical role of computers, which provide experimentalists with myriad measurements and endow theorists with the power to interpret them. Just half a century after the first astronomical tables emerged from clattering punched-card tabulators, the electronic computer has achieved something close to ubiquity in science. From the study of the heavens to investigations of the molecular basis of life itself, scientific endeavors have been changed forever.

A Machine to Unravel Matter

It is one of the more striking paradoxes of science that the investigation of nature's smallest constituents requires the largest of all instruments: accelerators that smash subatomic particles together at very high speed to unlock the secrets of matter. Physicists have been exploring the subatomic realm with particle accelerators for more than three decades. The deeper they probe, the more energetic the collisions must be. By the late 1990s, they hope to be looking into this microworld with a stupendous scientific tool called a supercollider. Resembling a series of linked racetracks, it will give a carefully regulated progression of electrical kicks to charged elementary particles until they are traveling almost at the speed of light—about 186,000 miles per second. When fully accelerated, particles will be directed head-on into each other, producing a shower of fragments that will provide valuable clues to the underlying structure of all things in the universe—and perhaps to the origins of the universe itself.

As explained on the following pages, computers will be critical at every stage of the supercollider's operation, from the timing of the electrical acceleration to the analysis of the particle-collision consequences. Controlling this multibillion-dollar research tool will be a truly awesome job. The planned supercollider has as its most ambitious feature a circular tunnel more than 50 miles long, and for the briefest instant, it will be able to release energy at a greater rate than could all the power plants on earth operating simultaneously.

A Giant to Penetrate the Subatomic World

A supercollider is really several accelerators—four in this example—combined in one huge facility and teamed in a relay of successively greater power and dimensions. Three of the accelerators add increasing amounts of energy to a stream of subatomic particles, simultaneously concentrating them into a narrow beam. When the particles are going fast enough, the beam is fed into a main collider ring for final acceleration and the collisions that reveal the particles' structure.

As particles in the main collider ring approach the velocity of light, they become progressively more difficult to divert from their naturally straight path into a curved one. The powerful magnets that are employed to influence the particles are strong enough only to steer them into the broadest of curves. For this reason, the main collider ring (opposite) must be so big that if it were built above ground, a viewer who was standing in the center could barely see it on the horizon.

Precise control is needed to send the particles to the right place at the right time at the right speed. The responsibility falls to a network of beam-position sensors connected to computers that continuously adjust magnet strength to focus the stream of particles into a beam less than 1/1,000 inch in diameter. Other computers check vacuum systems; they remove air from the pipe that contains the beam, permitting the particles to travel unimpeded around the rings. Additional computers monitor refrigeration units that keep the magnets cold (pages 112-113). Still others time the acceleration process to synchronize boosts in energy and shifts in paths until finally the particles meet in head-on collision.

Accelerating the particles and arranging collisions between them is only half the job. The other half—recording and analyzing the outcomes of the collisions—is an equally computer-intensive task. The collisions take place in interaction halls, each containing a huge electronic detector. It feeds signals to a complex of computers, which calculate the paths and energies of the particles generated in a collision, enabling scientists to identify them.

Interaction Hall

Interaction Hall

Against one wall of a protecting tunnel, the main collider ring carries two separate beams, stacked one above the other with their particles traveling in opposite directions. People and equipment move through the 10-foot-diameter tunnel on vehicles about the size of golf carts.

Accelerating Station

Small Booster Synchrotron

Linear Accelerator

Beam Source

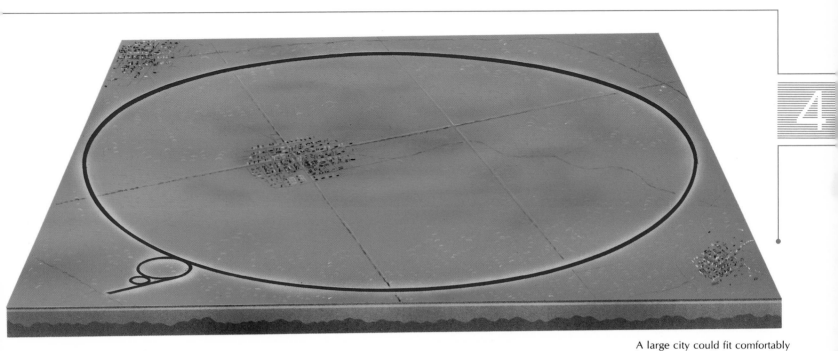

A large city could fit comfortably within the main collider ring, which lies out of sight 20 feet or more underground, buried to minimize radiation hazards. Three smaller accelerators, drawn to scale at lower left, feed particles into the main ring.

Interaction Hall

Main Collider Ring

Interaction Hall

Accelerating Station

Large Booster Synchrotron

Arrows trace the beam path. From its source *(far left),* the beam is accelerated in a straight-line, or linear, accelerator, then fed into a circular synchrotron, where energy is almost doubled by jolts from the accelerating station. The single beam becomes two as it is sent alternately in one direction and then the other around the larger synchrotron, which raises energy 1,000 times. Finally, in the main ring, energy increases twentyfold and the beams cross to collide nearly head on.

Getting the Beam up to Speed

Particles in this collider beam start out as a puff of hydrogen gas that is barely moving. In order for fruitful collisions to take place, the nuclei of hydrogen atoms must be accelerated to nearly the velocity of light. Because the nuclei have an electrical charge, they can be speeded up in stages by repeated applications of electrical force, which are represented in the drawings of the acceleration process immediately below as plus signs and minus signs.

The particle stream is not continuous; instead, the particles travel in bunches that are separately accelerated. This occurs

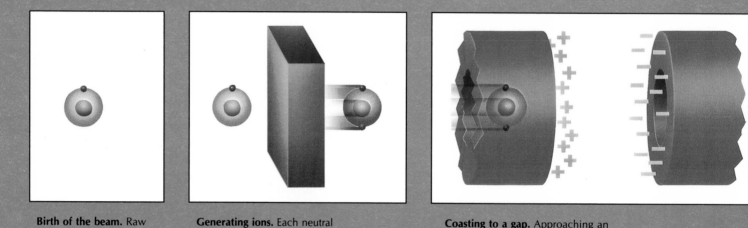

Birth of the beam. Raw material for the beam is hydrogen gas—here, a single atom. Each atom—a central proton, positively charged, and a negatively charged electron—is electrically neutral.

Generating ions. Each neutral hydrogen atom is made into an ion—in this case, a proton with two electrons—having a net negative charge. First, an electric arc liberates the positively charged protons. Each proton then gains two electrons when it strikes a metal surface.

Coasting to a gap. Approaching an acceleration gap, a negative ion of the linear accelerator beam is shielded from the electric force as it flies through a drift tube. If the ion were at the gap, it would be slowed instead of speeded, attracted and thus retarded by the positive charge at the near side of the gap.

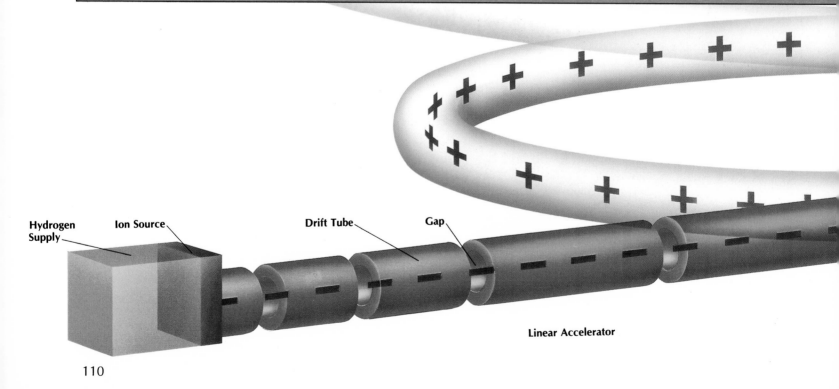

Hydrogen Supply

Ion Source

Drift Tube

Gap

Linear Accelerator

as they pass through a series of straight pipes called drift tubes, which are separated by narrow gaps. As a bunch of particles crosses each gap, it is repulsed by an electrical force from behind and attracted by an opposite electrical force ahead. Once it is within a tube, it is protected from electrical charge. This is necessary because the electrical field at the gap has to rapidly reverse itself—at the rate of several million times every second—to prevent any current from arcing across the narrow divide. Yet the field must have the correct direction at the precise instant the particles emerge from the tubes; otherwise, they would be slowed or deflected rather than accelerated. Only a computer could manage such exquisite synchronization.

A further feat of precise timing occurs as the particles pass out of the linear accelerator and into the first booster ring: They must arrive just in time to join one of the bunches already circling there at very high speed. In this manner, the bunches are built up in density to seven billion particles to ensure a high probability of collision when the acceleration process is complete.

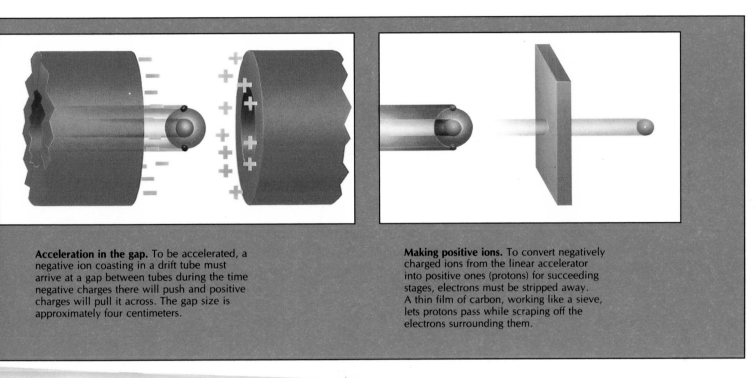

Acceleration in the gap. To be accelerated, a negative ion coasting in a drift tube must arrive at a gap between tubes during the time negative charges there will push and positive charges will pull it across. The gap size is approximately four centimeters.

Making positive ions. To convert negatively charged ions from the linear accelerator into positive ones (protons) for succeeding stages, electrons must be stripped away. A thin film of carbon, working like a sieve, lets protons pass while scraping off the electrons surrounding them.

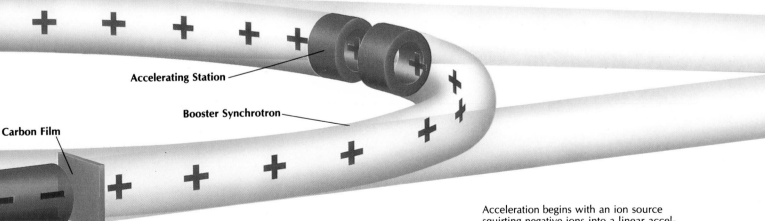

Accelerating Station

Booster Synchrotron

Carbon Film

Acceleration begins with an ion source squirting negative ions into a linear accelerator. Ions gain speed at gaps between drift tubes, the lengths of which increase with the growing velocity of the ions. A film of carbon turns negative ions into protons just after they enter the booster synchrotron; there the protons pick up energy each time they pass through an accelerating station similar to a short section of a linear accelerator.

Beam Pipe

Liquid Helium

Liquid Helium

Superconducting Coil

Liquid Helium

Iron Yoke

Liquid Nitrogen

Insulation

Helium Gas

In the main collider ring, two proton beams—
streaming in opposite directions—travel
in pipes surrounded by magnet coils that are
chilled by liquid helium and nitrogen to
carry electricity without any losses. A heavy
iron yoke increases magnetic strength. Two
kinds of magnets are used. A dipole magnet
(blue), with one north and one south pole,
keeps the particles on a circular path; a
quadrupole *(red)*—rather like two dipoles set
side by side, north pole to south pole—
focuses the particles into a narrow beam.

Switching to a New Track

To transfer a beam from one booster synchrotron to the
next, special magnets *(green)* nudge the protons into
a transfer line connecting the two. A similar extraction
system switches beams into the main ring and dumps them
in an emergency. The magnetic bending (exaggerated in
the drawing for clarity) takes place in stages, beginning
with a magnet called a kicker that shoves the protons just
far enough out of their circular path to place them under
the influence of the following two magnets. These
devices, called septum magnets, continue bending the
beam into its new direction. Kicker and septum magnets
alike turn on instantly when a control computer decides
to extract the beam from the synchrotron, but they remain
off at other times so that they do not disrupt the normal
path of the beam. Another bending magnet—named a
Lambertson magnet after its designer—is far enough from
the accelerator beam to be on all the time.

Chilled Magnets to Guide the Beam

Some of the biggest and strongest electromagnets ever produced are planned for the supercollider. Their function is to guide speeding protons along a roughly circular course in the boosters and main ring *(left)*, to shift beams between accelerators *(bottom)* and to focus the beams tightly for the maximum number of collisions.

An accelerator's electromagnets, like those found in doorbells, consist of current-carrying coils of wire. However, the magnetic strength needed for the main collider ring is so great that ordinary electromagnets cannot readily supply it. Built with such magnets, a supercollider would be much larger than 50 miles in circumference and would consume four billion watts,

enough power to light up Washington, D.C., four times over.

To save on construction costs and conserve electricity, superconducting magnets are planned. Their coils are kept so cold by liquid helium and liquid nitrogen that resistance to electricity disappears; the current and the resulting magnetic pull, once started, will continue indefinitely without dissipating. The only electric power needed, after the brief start-up, is the wattage necessary to refrigerate the helium and nitrogen, less than one percent of the amount that would be used without superconductivity.

Should a temperature rise in a magnet coil cause it to lose superconductivity, heat generated by the immense current flowing through the coil would destroy the magnet in less than a tenth of a second. The uncontrolled proton beam would career into the wall of the beam pipe, causing damage. To prevent this catastrophe, thousands of microcomputers are positioned around the ring. At the first sign of overheating in a coil, a nearby microcomputer instantly shunts the current around the threatened magnet before it can be destroyed, while another computer diverts the beam out of the ring.

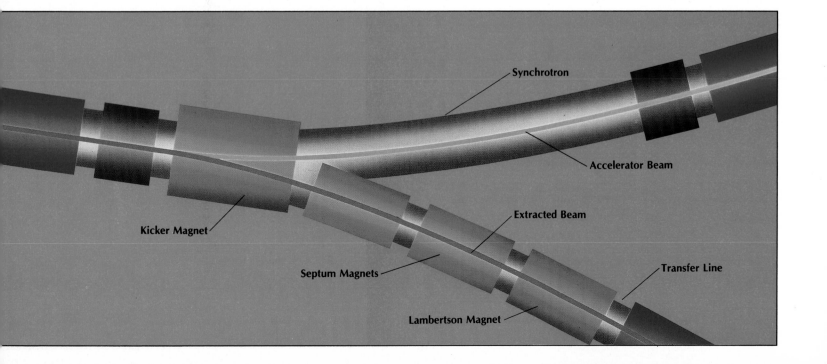

Synchrotron

Accelerator Beam

Kicker Magnet

Extracted Beam

Septum Magnets

Transfer Line

Lambertson Magnet

Giant Detectors for Tiny Particles

The huge dimensions of this supercollider's main ring extend to all its components, including the instruments in the interaction halls that gauge the results of proton collision. Sensitive tracking devices and energy detectors containing great masses of iron are needed to identify and trap the evanescent products of intersecting beams. A typical assemblage of trackers and detectors (below) weighs 50,000 tons and stands about 60 feet tall. The number of collisions to be registered is equally outsize—100 million every second.

The job of computers in the interaction halls is to monitor the proceedings. Computer tasks include discarding most of the data from the collisions—repetitions of phenomena already well known. The screening, called triggering, begins with storing all the signals from the instrument in electronic circuits. The data is held there, in the analog form of varying electric currents, long enough for special computers built into the trackers and detectors to decide which of the signals to throw away and which to keep for closer study. The data preserved in this step is then converted to digital form, examined and, again, either kept or discarded. This filtering process continues by stages, each one requiring a more detailed look at the data that has passed previous levels of triggering. For example, a trigger computer might be programmed to calculate part of an interesting particle's path, then compare the result with other paths that are stored in memory to decide whether the data should be tossed out or passed on to the next higher trigger.

At the top of the triggering hierarchy, phalanxes of microcomputers work in parallel, all operating simultaneously while each handles a different part of the information. Surviving data is recorded on magnetic tape or optical disks and goes to a central computer facility for final analysis. Of all the collisions that occur each second, fewer than 10 provide data that reaches the tape.

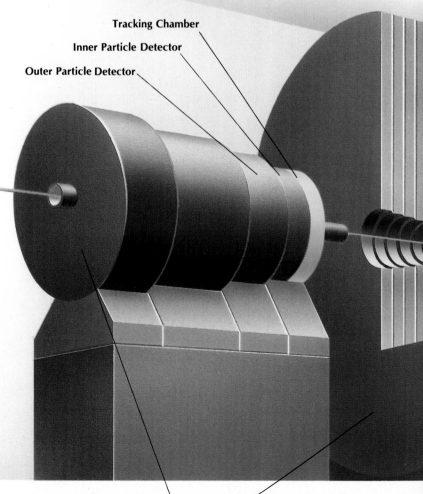

Tracking Chamber

Inner Particle Detector

Outer Particle Detector

Muon Detectors

To identify and measure all particles created when two protons collide, the detector uses two major types of components. A tracking chamber (yellow) measures the curved paths taken by electrically charged particles under the magnetic influence of a superconducting coil (purple). Layers surrounding the tracking chamber measure the total energy of individual particles or clusters of closely spaced particles, both charged and neutral. Inner layers detect lightweight particles such as electrons; outer layers stop heavy particles such as mesons and protons. These layers also indicate particles' direction of motion. In the outermost layers, iron plates about three feet thick are separated by special tracking chambers. This multilayered sandwich detects muons, the heavy, high-energy cousins of the electron. One inscrutable collision "particle"—the weightless, chargeless neutrino—escapes detection; its presence is inferred from the energy missing after everything else has been accounted for.

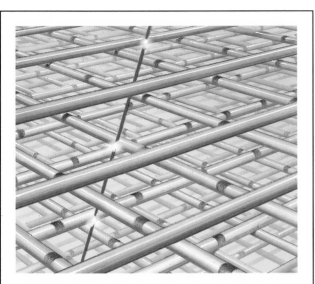

Tracing paths. A tracking chamber contains a gas and wires. When a high-energy particle enters, it rips electrons from the gas molecules it passes, creating bursts of electric charge that are picked up by the nearest wire. These bursts send signals that a computer interprets as points in the particle's trajectory.

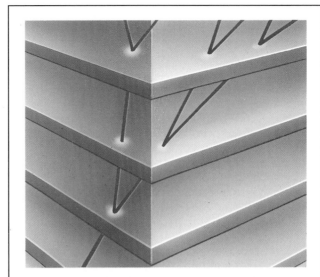

Gauging energy. A particle transiting an energy detector strikes sheets of a heavy metal such as uranium, giving up some of its energy to particles created by the impact. A liquid between sheets is used to gauge the energy of all the particles; summing energies from all the layers gives the energy of the original particle.

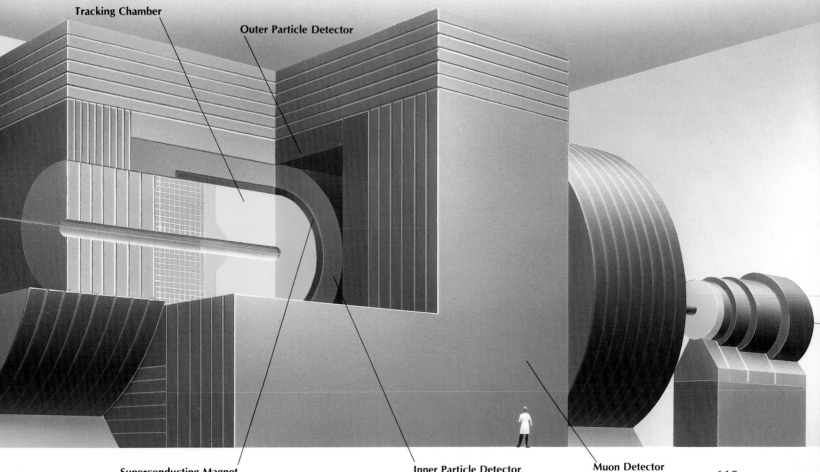

Tracking Chamber

Outer Particle Detector

Superconducting Magnet

Inner Particle Detector

Muon Detector

A Burst
of Particles

The herculean task of making sense of data produced by a supercollider is suggested at right in a computer simulation of the paths taken by more than 100 of the particles generated when the energies of two speeding protons are released. This picture results from analysis of energy-detector data as well as tracking-chamber data, consisting of a huge and confusing collection of unconnected dots. Which dots belong together in which path must be figured out by computer, using pattern-recognition programs to connect the dots into trajectories.

Trajectories alone cannot identify all the collision particles and gauge their energies, although they give some of this information. A curved track, for example, means that the particle is electrically charged. The direction of curvature indicates the kind of charge; in this reconstruction, clockwise curvature denotes positive charge. The amount of curvature is also a measure of particle energy, for the magnet bends low-energy particles into tighter curves than it does high-energy particles.

All but the lowest energy particles pass entirely through the tracking chamber into the energy detectors, which provide the rest of the data needed. A particle having so much energy that it penetrates to the special tracking chambers and iron plates in the outermost layers of the detector assembly is assumed to be a muon.

Most of the collision particles identified in this way are not the ones that make up the innermost structure of matter. Those particles have very short lives when generated, changing into other particles too quickly to be detected. Their presence must be inferred from the patterns of the more stable and ordinary particles into which they decay. Only in this round-about way can scientists get at the elusive answers they seek.

How the tracks of collision particles reveal their nature is indicated in this computer reconstruction. Nearly circular tracks—most of which emanate from the center of the starburst, where two protons collided—are low-energy particles (1). Curved lines are medium-energy particles (2). Solid straight tracks are really slightly curved and represent high-energy charged particles (3). Dotted straight tracks represent particles that, having no electric charge, are not recorded in the tracking chamber; the computer infers the lines from energy data (4). Tracks that miss the starburst are particles that emerge from decaying products of the original collision. (5)

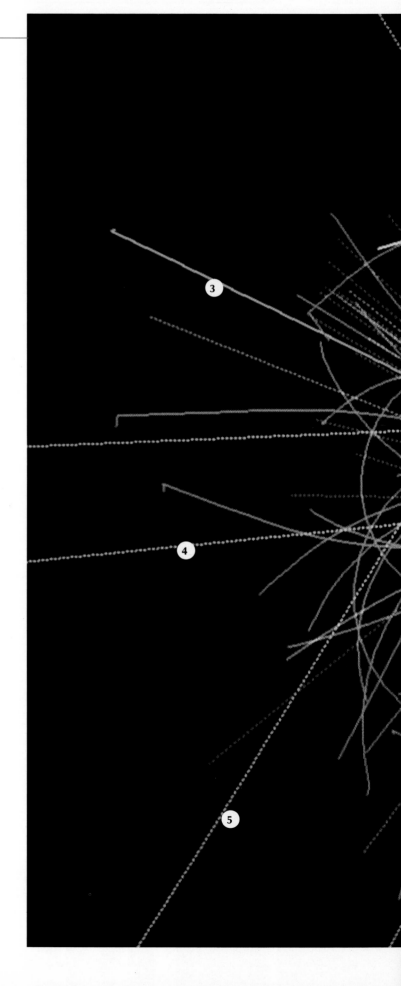

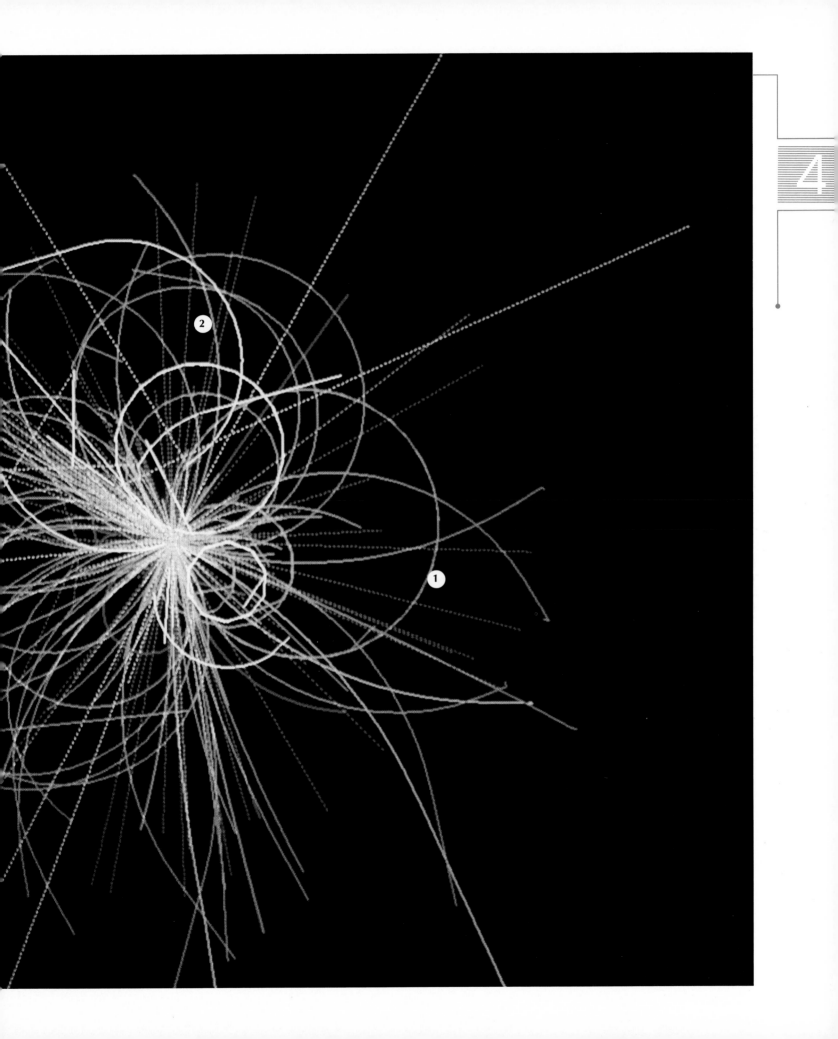

Glossary

Algorithm: a step-by-step procedure for solving a problem.

Amino acids: the building blocks of proteins.

Amplitude: the maximum value for a periodic wave; half the peak-to-trough value.

Analog: the representation of a continuously changing physical variable (sound, for example) by another physical variable (such as electrical current).

Analog-to-digital converter: a device that changes an analog signal into digital information.

Arithmetic logic unit: the part of the central processor that performs arithmetic operations such as subtraction and logical operations such as TRUE-FALSE comparisons.

Assembler: a program that converts the mnemonic instructions of assembly-language programs into the zeros and ones of binary machine code.

Assembly language: a low-level programming language, specific to a given computer, that uses short mnemonics corresponding directly to machine instructions and that allows a programmer to use symbolic addresses.

Atom: the smallest component of an element; consists of protons and neutrons surrounded by a cloud of electrons.

Bit: the smallest unit of information in a computer, equivalent to a single zero or one. The word "bit" is a contraction of "binary digit."

Byte: a sequence of bits, usually eight, treated as a unit for computation or storage.

Cathode-ray tube (CRT): a TV-like display device with a screen that lights up where it is struck from the inside by a beam of electrons.

Celestial mechanics: the study of the motion of stars and planets.

Compiler: a computer program that converts software written in a high-level language into either machine code or assembly language; the compiled program is stored for use at a later time.

Copernican theory: the theory that the earth and other planets revolve around the sun.

Cosmology: the study of the origin and evolution of the universe.

Crystal: a solid that has a regularly repeating internal arrangement of atoms.

Digital: pertaining to the representation or transmission of data by discrete signals.

Distributed control: a set of programs, each with its own specific function, interconnected to carry out an integrated function.

Double precision: the use of two computer words to represent a number.

Electromechanical: composed of both electrical and mechanical, or moving, parts; most early computers were electromechanical devices.

Electron: a negatively charged particle that orbits the nucleus of an atom.

Electron density: the number of electrons per unit of volume.

Electron density map: a representation of electron density at various points in a crystal structure.

Evolution: the theory that life on earth developed gradually from simple to more complex organisms.

Fast Fourier transform: a computational technique used to speed the conversion of complex waves and signals into their simpler components.

Floating-point notation: a method of expressing numbers as a product of a fraction and a base number raised to a certain power; so named because the decimal point moves, or floats, depending on the size of the exponent: For instance, 93,000,000 can become either $.93 \times 10^8$ or $.093 \times 10^9$. Floating-point notation allows computers to work with very large and very small figures by reducing the number of digits needed to represent them.

FORTRAN: a computer language used primarily for scientific or algebraic purposes.

Frequency: the number of times per second that a wave cycle (one peak and one trough) repeats.

Hardware: the physical apparatus of a computer system.

Hypothesis: an idea or supposition to be tested in an experiment.

Ion: an atom or molecule that has a net negative or positive electric charge.

Kernel: The most basic section of the UNIX operating system. It manages the storage of data, organizes tasks and handles peripheral devices.

Language: a set of rules or conventions to describe a process to a computer.

LINC: acronym for Laboratory Instrument Computer; a computer introduced in 1962 for the control and analysis of experimental processes.

LISP: (for List Processing) a language that is based on the manipulation of lists of data.

Machine code: a set of binary digits that can be directly understood by a computer without translation.

Magnetic tape: plastic tape coated with a magnetic material on which information can be stored.

Mainframe computer: the largest type of computer, usually capable of serving many users simultaneously, with a processing speed about 100 times faster than that of a microcomputer.

Memory: the principal space inside a computer for storing instructions and data.

Microcomputer: a portable computer, based on a microprocessor and intended for use by an individual; often called a personal computer.

Microprocessor: a single chip containing all the elements of a computer's central processing unit; sometimes called a computer on a chip.

Microwave: an electromagnetic wave in the radio frequency spectrum above one gigahertz, or a billion cycles per second.

Minicomputer: a midsize computer smaller than a mainframe and usually with much more memory than a personal computer.

Model: a computer program that simulates complex physical phenomena through the manipulation of mathematical equations.

Molecule: the smallest unit of a chemical compound that can exist independently. Molecules usually are made up of many atoms bound together.

Monte Carlo method: a procedure that uses random sampling in order to approximate the solution of a problem; the Monte Carlo method is employed when the problem is too complex for a mathematical solution.

Mutation: a change in an organism's genes or chromosomes.

Neutron: a subparticle of an atom with no charge; a constituent of all atomic nuclei except hydrogen.

Nuclear fission: the process of splitting apart the nucleus of an atom.

Nuclear fusion: the combination of two atomic nuclei to form a heavier nucleus.

Nuclear physics: a branch of physics that deals with the behavior, structure and component parts of atomic nuclei.

Number crunching: the processing of large amounts of data.

On line: immediately accessible by a computer's central processing unit. Refers to the technique of entering data and instructions directly into a computer.

Operating system: a set of programs used to control, assist or supervise all other programs that run on a computer system.

Optics: the study of phenomena associated with visible and invisible light and with vision.

Oscillation: a complete cycle of a regularly repeating motion; for example, the oscillation of a pendulum is one round trip from its original position.

Oscilloscope: an output device that displays a signal in wave form on a CRT.

Particle collider: a machine, often called an atom smasher, that physicists use to explore the components of atoms.

Peripheral: a device that is attached to a computer; it includes all input/output devices and data storage devices.

Pipe: to take the output of one command or program and feed it directly into another command or program.

Plasma: a state of matter consisting of free atomic nuclei and electrons.

Potentiometer: a mechanically variable resistor that can control electrical voltages.

Program: a set of instructions for performing an operation or solving a problem by computer.

Proteins: a family of complex molecules that play a variety of roles within the cell.

Proton: one of three particle types (the neutron and electron are the others) that make up an atom; a hydrogen atom is composed of one proton with one electron orbiting around it.

Pseudorandom numbers: a series of numbers produced by programs called random-number generators; described as "pseudo" because they are created by a fixed procedure and thus are not truly random.

Punched card: a rectangular card on which data is represented as holes.

Random-number generator: a computer program that produces a scrambled series of numbers appearing to have no relationship to one another.

Real-time processing: computer processing rapid enough to solve problems and handle events as they occur.

Relay: a device that makes or breaks one or more connections in an electric circuit.

Rounding: a process for shortening a number; if the leftmost digit of those to be shed is equal to or greater than 5, the rightmost digit that remains after rounding is increased by 1, otherwise the rightmost digit is left unchanged.

Satellite altimetry: measuring the height of earth features, land or sea, from a satellite.

Seismic imaging: the use of reflected sound waves to create a picture of rock layers below the surface of the earth and beneath the ocean floor.

Seismology: the study of the depths of the earth through natural and artificial seismic signals.

Sensor: an information-pickup device that converts physical energy such as temperature or light into electrical signals, which may then be translated for use by the computer.

Shell: A UNIX program that manages the interaction between the system and user; it interprets requests from the user, calls up programs from memory and executes them.

Simulation: the representation of the behavior of a real system with a computer model.

Software: programs that enable a computer to perform various tasks; contrasted with hardware, or the actual computer apparatus.

Supercomputer: a term applied to the fastest, most powerful computers at a given time; supercomputers typically are used to solve scientific problems that involve the creation of mathematical models and the manipulation of large amounts of data.

Superconductor: a material that, at low temperatures, can conduct a current with no electrical resistance.

Superminicomputer: a minicomputer that has a particularly large memory.

Synchrotron: a ring-shaped accelerator of a particle collider; magnets steer the particles in a circle so that they repeatedly enter a section that gives the particles an additional boost of energy.

Tabulator: a machine that processes punched cards.

Tectonic plates: blocks of the earth's crust that "float" on the molten rock below and move more or less independently; the grinding at the borders of the seven major plates produces earthquakes.

Terminal: A keyboard and display unit (usually a CRT) through which a person communicates with a computer.

Time sharing: the simultaneous use of a computer by more than one person.

Truncation: the process of dropping digits from a number in order to fit it into the word size of a particular computer's circuits.

UNIX: a general-purpose, multiuser, interactive, time-sharing operating system popular within education and research institutions.

Word: the number of bits that a computer can store at a single memory location, treated by the computer as a unit; word size ranges from eight bits in a microcomputer to as many as 64 bits in a supercomputer.

X-rays: electromagnetic radiation, much shorter in wavelength than light, that is capable of penetrating solids.

Bibliography

Books

Atkinson, Kendall, *Elementary Numerical Analysis*. New York: John Wiley & Sons, 1985.

Baehne, G. W., ed., *Practical Applications of the Punched Card Method in Colleges and Universities*. New York: Columbia University Press, 1935.

Bartlett, John, *Familiar Quotations*. Boston: Little, Brown and Company, 1980.

Bashe, Charles J., et al., *IBM's Early Computers*. Cambridge: The MIT Press, 1986.

Bell, C. Gordon, J. Craig Mudge and John E. McNamara, *Computer Engineering*. Bedford, Mass.: Digital Press, 1978.

Belzer, Jack, Albert G. Holzman and Allen Kent, *Encyclopedia of Computer Science and Technology*. New York: Marcel Dekker, Inc., 1975.

Biographical Memoirs. Vol. 32. New York: Columbia University Press, 1958.

Blundell, T. L., and L. N. Johnson, *Protein Crystallography*. New York: Academic Press, 1976.

Bolt, Bruce A., *Earthquakes: A Primer*. San Francisco: W. H. Freeman and Company, 1978.

Bolter, J. David, *Turing's Man: Western Culture in the Computer Age*. Chapel Hill, N.C.: The University of North Carolina Press, 1984.

Bourne, S. J., *The UNIX System*. Reading, Mass.: Addison-Wesley, 1982.

Brennan, Jean Ford, *The IBM Watson Laboratory at Columbia University: A History*. Armonk, N.Y.: International Business Machines, 1971.

Brigham, E. Oran, *The Fast Fourier Transform*. Englewood Cliffs, N.J.: Prentice-Hall, 1973.

Brillinger, David R., ed., *The Collected Works of John W. Tukey*. Vol. 2. Monterey, Calif.: Wadsworth Advanced Books & Software, 1984.

Chirlian, Paul M., *Understanding Computers*. Beaverton, Ore.: Dilithium Press, 1978.

Dickerson, Richard E., and Irving Geis, *The Structure and Action of Proteins*. New York: Harper & Row, 1969.

Duncan, John Charles, *Astronomy: A Textbook*. New York: Harper & Brothers, 1955.

Eckert, W. J., *Punched Card Methods in Scientific Computation*. Cambridge: The MIT Press, 1940.

Eckhouse, Richard H., Jr., *Minicomputer Systems: Organization and Programming (PDP-11)*. Englewood Cliffs, N.J.: Prentice-Hall, 1975.

Educational Research Forum Proceedings. New York: International Business Machines, 1947.

El-Asfouri, Souhail, Olin Johnson and Willis K. King, *Computer Organization and Programming: VAX-11*. Reading, Mass.: Addison-Wesley, 1984.

Fernbach, S., and A. Taub, eds., *Computers and Their Role in the Physical Sciences*. New York: Gordon and Breach Science, 1970.

Garrison, Paul, *Programming the TI-59 & the HP-41 Calculators*. Blue Ridge Summit, Pa.: Tab Books, 1982.

Gillispie, Charles Coulston, ed., *Dictionary of Scientific Biography*. Vols. 5 and 7. New York: Charles Scribner's Sons, 1981.

Glusker, Jenny Pickworth, and Kenneth N. Trueblood, *Crystal Structure Analysis: A Primer*. New York: Oxford University Press, 1985.

Goldstine, Herman H., *The Computer: From Pascal to Von Neumann*. Princeton, N.J.: Princeton University Press, 1972.

Groff, James R., and Paul Weinberg, *Understanding UNIX: A Conceptual Guide*. Indianapolis: Que Corporation, 1984.

Halsey, William, and Emanuel Friedman, eds., *Collier's Encyclopedia*. New York: Macmillan Educational Co., 1982.

Hammersley, J. M., and D. C. Handscomb, *Monte Carlo Methods*. New York: John Wiley & Sons, 1964.

Hanks, Thomas C., *The National Earthquake Hazards Reduction Program—Scientific Status*. (U.S. Geological Survey Bulletin 1659.) Washington: U.S. Government Printing Office, 1985.

Hewlett, William R., *Inventions of Opportunity: Matching Technology with Market Needs*. Palo Alto, Calif.: Hewlett-Packard, 1983.

Iacopi, Robert, *Earthquake Country*. Menlo Park, Calif.: Lane Books, 1971.

Judson, Horace Freeland, *The Eighth Day of Creation*. New York: Simon and Schuster, 1979.

Knuth, Donald E., *The Art of Computer Programming*. Reading, Mass.: Addison-Wesley, 1971.

Ledley, Robert Steven, *Use of Computers in Biology and Medicine*. New York: McGraw-Hill, 1965.

Moran, Emilio F., ed., *The Ecosystem Concept in Anthropology*. Boulder, Colo.: Westview Press, 1984.

National Earthquake Hazards Reduction Program: Fiscal Year 1985 Activities. (A Report to the United States Congress.) Washington: U.S. Government Printing Office, 1986.

Nelson, H. Roice, Jr., *New Technologies in Exploration Geophysics*. Houston, Tex.: Gulf Publishing Company, 1983.

Ortega, James M., ed., *Computer Science and Scientific Computing*. New York: Academic Press, 1976.

Pavelle, Richard, ed., *Applications of Computer Algebra*. Boston: Kluwer Academic Publishers, 1985.

Pratt, D. J., and M. D. Gwynne, *Rangeland Management and Ecology in East Africa*. Huntington, N.Y.: Robert E. Krieger Publishing Company, 1977.

Press, Frank, and Raymond Siever, *Earth*. San Francisco: W. H. Freeman and Company, 1978.

Rabiner, Lawrence R., and Charles M. Rader, eds., *Digital Signal Processing*. New York: IEEE Press, 1972.

Ralston, A., ed. *Encyclopedia of Computer Science*. New York: Petrocelli/Charter, 1983.

Ralston, Anthony, and Edwin D. Reilly Jr., eds., *The Encyclopedia of Computer Science and Engineering*. New York: Van Nostrand Reinhold Company, 1983.

Rodgers, William, *Think*. New York: Stein and Day, 1969.

Schmidt, Charles W., and Cyril D. Curtis, "A 50-mA Negative Hydrogen-Ion Source." *The Proceedings of the 1979 Particle Accelerator Conference*. San Francisco, 1979.

Shapiro, Harvey Lee, *Assembler Language Programming for the PDP-11*. Palo Alto, Calif.: Mayfield Publishing, 1984.

Sobel, Robert, *I.B.M.: Colossus in Transition*. New York: Bantam Books, 1981.

Stacy, Ralph W., and Bruce D. Waxman, *Computers in Biomedical Research*. Vol. 2. New York: Academic Press, 1965.

Streeter, Donald N., *The Scientific Process and the Computer*. New York: John Wiley & Sons, 1974.

Struve, Otto, *Elementary Astronomy*. New York: Oxford University Press, 1959.

Taub, A. H., ed., *John von Neumann Collected Works*. Vol. 5. New York: Pergamon Press, 1963.

Ulam, S. M., *Adventures of a Mathematician*. New York: Charles Scribner's Sons, 1976.

Walker, Bryce, and the Editors of Time-Life Books, *Earthquake* (The Planet Earth series). Alexandria, Va.: Time-Life Books, 1982.

Williams, Michael R., *A History of Computing Technology*. Englewood Cliffs, N.J.: Prentice-Hall, 1985.

Periodicals

Adams, Jeanne, et al., "Institutionalization of FORTRAN." *Annals of the History of Computing*, Jan. 1984.

Alsop, Ronald, "Scientists Are Turning to Computers in Search for New Chemicals, Drugs." *Wall Street Journal*, Aug. 23, 1983.

Anderson, Don L., and Adam M. Dziewonski, "Seismic Tomography." *Scientific American*, Oct. 1984.

Angier, Natalie, "The Colossus of Colliders." *Time*, Nov. 11, 1985.

"An Approach to Complexity: Numerical Computations." *Science*, Apr. 26, 1985.

Archuleta, Ralph J., "A Faulting Model for the 1979 Imperial Valley Earthquake." *Journal of Geophysical Research*, June 10, 1984.

Backus, John, et al., "Early Days of FORTRAN." *Annals of the History of Computing*, Jan. 1984.

Bashe, Charles J., "The SSEC in Historical Perspective." *Annals of the History of Computing*, Oct. 1982.

Beard, Kenneth V., "Oscillation Models for Predicting Raindrop Axis and Backscatter Ratios." *Radio Science*, Jan.-Feb. 1984.

The Bell System Technical Journal, July-Aug. 1978.

Bogert, Dixon, "The Fermilab Accelerator Control System." *Nuclear Instruments and Methods in Physics Research*, 1986.

Bonner, Michael K., "Accelerator Tries for 2-TeV Level." *Research and Development*, Nov. 1984.

Bragg, Lawrence, "X-Ray Crystallography." *Scientific American*, July 1968.

Broad, William J., "Atom-Smashing Now and in the Future: A New Era Begins." *New York Times*, Feb. 3, 1987.

Brodeur, Paul, "In the Face of Doubt." *The New Yorker*, June 9, 1986.

"The Computer Issue." *Science*, Apr. 26, 1985.

Comrie, L. J., "Anecdotes." *Annals of the History of Computing*, Oct. 1983.

Conn, Robert W., "The Engineering of Magnetic Fusion Reactors." *Scientific American*, Oct. 1983.

Cook, Frederick A., Larry D. Brown and Jack E. Oliver, "The Southern Appalachians and the Growth of Continents." *Scientific American*, July 1986.

Coppi, Bruno, and Jan Rem, "The Tokamak Approach in Fusion Research." *Scientific American*, July 1972.

Coppock, D. L., J. E. Ellis and David Swift:
"Livestock Feeding Ecology and Resource Utilization in a Nomadic Pastoral Ecosystem." *Journal of Applied Ecology*, 1986.
"Seasonal Nutritional Characteristics of Livestock Diets in a Nomadic Pastoral Ecosystem." *Journal of Applied Ecology*, 1986.

Coughenour, M. B., et al., "Energy Extraction and Use in a Nomadic Pastoral Ecosystem." *Science*, Nov. 8, 1985.

Diebold, Robert, "Computing Needs of the Superconducting Super Collider." *Transactions of Nuclear Science*, 1985.

Dollotta, Ted, "Interview with Eric Schmidt." *UNIX Review*, Oct. 1986.

Durham, Tony, "A High-Energy Solution for Physicists." *Computing Magazine*, July 3, 1986.

Eckert, W. J., "Electrons and Computation." *The Scientific Monthly*, Nov. 1948.

Felsenfeld, Gary, "DNA." *Scientific American*, Oct. 1985.

Fiedler, David:
"UNIX: The Easy Way." *Computers & Electronics*, Sept. 1983.
"The UNIX Tutorial, Part 1.: An Introduction to Features and Facilities." *BYTE*, Aug. 1983.

"The Five Best-Managed Companies." *Dun's Review*, Dec. 1975.

Fowler, T. K., and Richard F. Post, "Progress Toward Fusion Power." *Scientific American*, Dec. 1966.

Garred, Eileen, "Harvard-Made Detector Used in First Test of Giant Accelerator." *Harvard Gazette*, Nov. 1, 1987.

"Getting the Drop on 'Giant' Rain." *Science News*, Nov. 1, 1986.

Grosch, H.R.J., Review of *Punched Card Methods in Scientific Computation*, by Wallace J. Eckert. *Annals of the History of Computing*, Oct. 1985.

Hertzberger, L. O., and W. Hoogland, eds., "The Fermilab

Advanced Computer Program Multi-Microprocessor Project." *Computing in High Energy Physics* (Amsterdam: North-Holland), 1986.

Hughes, Ernest S., "The SSEC and Its Carry-Over Effects on the IBM Type 650." *Annals of the History of Computing,* Jan. 1986.

Hurd, Cuthbert C., "A Note on Early Monte Carlo Computations and Scientific Meetings." *Annals of the History of Computing,* Apr. 1985.

IEEE Transactions on Audio and Electroacoustics, June 1969.

Jackson, J. David, Maury Tigner and Stanley Wojcicki, "The Superconducting Supercollider." *Scientific American,* Mar. 1986.

Keating, Barry, "Computer Simulations: Put the Real World in Your Computer." *Creative Computing,* Nov. 1985.

Lederman, Leon M., "The Superconducting Super Accelerator." *Research and Development,* Feb. 1985.

Lee, J.A.N., "An Annotated Bibliography of FORTRAN." *Annals of the History of Computing,* Jan. 1984.

Levine, Ronald D., "Supercomputers." *Scientific American,* Jan. 1982.

Lewin, Roger, "Computers Track the Path of Plant Evolution." *Science,* Mar. 11, 1983.

McIlroy, M. D., "The UNIX Success Story." *UNIX Review,* Oct. 1986.

McKean, Kevin, "The Orderly Pursuit of Pure Disorder." *Discover,* Jan. 1987.

McPherson, John C., et al., "A Large-Scale, General-Purpose Electronic Digital Calculator—The SSEC." *Annals of the History of Computing,* Oct. 1982.

"Mapping the Ocean Floor by Satellite." *U.S. News & World Report,* Mar. 3, 1986.

Marsh, James G., "Global Mean Sea Surface Based upon the Seasat Altimeter Data." *Journal of Geophysical Research,* Mar. 10, 1986.

Martin, Charles L., ed., "AT&T Enters the Market." *Personal Computing,* July 1984.

"Meetings in Retrospect." *Annals of the History of Computing,* Apr. 1982.

Metropolis, Nicholas, and Eldred C. Nelson, "Early Computing at Los Alamos." *Annals of the History of Computing,* Oct. 1982.

Mims, Forrest M., III, "The Computer Scientist: Random Numbers." *Computers & Electronics,* Nov. 1984.

Mistry, Nariman B., Ronald A. Poling and Edward H. Thorndike, "Particles with Naked Beauty." *Scientific American,* July 1983.

Monthly Notices of the Royal Astronomical Society. London: Royal Astronomical Society, May 1932.

Mooers, C.N.K., et al., "The Potential of Satellite-Based Radar Altimeters." *EOS Transactions, American Geophysical Union,* Mar. 6, 1984.

Mosaic, Vol. 17, No. 1, 1986.

Mosaic, Vol.16, No.3, 1985.

Mutter, John C., "Seismic Images of Plate Boundaries." *Scientific American,* Feb. 1986.

Newsweek, Feb. 9, 1948.

Niklas, Karl, "Computer-Simulated Plant Evolution." *Scientific American,* Mar. 1986.

Patrusky, Ben, "Biology's Computational Future." *Mosaic,* winter 1985.

Peterson, Ivars:
  "Raindrop Oscillations." *Science News,* Mar. 2, 1985.
  "Rolling Rocks and Tumbling Dice." *Science News,* May 3, 1986.

Phelps, Byron E., "Early Electronic Computer Developments at IBM." *Annals of the History of Computing,* July 1980.

Raugh, Michael R., "Modeling California Earthquakes and Earth Structures." *Communications of the ACM,* Nov. 1985.

Reiter, Carla, "Toy Universes." *Science 86,* June 1986.

"Reports: Seasat Mission Overview." *Science,* June 29, 1979.

Saunders, Rob, "Making UNIX Secure." *BYTE,* Apr. 1986.

Scientific American, Dec. 1981.

"Sea-Surface Shape by Satellite." *Science News,* Jan. 18, 1986.

"Seismic Processing Overview." *Cray Channels,* Vol. 5, No. 2, no date.

Spitzer, Lyman, Jr., "The Stellarator." *Scientific American,* Oct. 1958.

Surko, C. M., and R. E. Slusher, "Waves and Turbulence in a Tokamak Fusion Plasma." *Science,* Aug. 26, 1983.

Sutton, Christine, "A Triumph for Superconductors." *New Scientist,* July 21, 1983.

Sykes, Lynn R., and Jack F. Evernden, "The Verification of a Comprehensive Nuclear Test Ban." *Scientific American,* Oct. 1982.

Thomsen, Dietrick E.:
  "Annihilations at 2 Trillion Volts." *Science News,* Sept. 28, 1985.
  "Schrodinger Goes to Monte Carlo." *Science News,* Aug. 23, 1986.

"Too Long with a Good Thing." *Forbes,* Apr. 15, 1968.

Tropp, Henry S., "Origin of the Term *Bit*." *Annals of the History of Computing,* Apr. 1984.

Von Baeyer, Hans Christian, "Physika: The Odds Against Order." *The Sciences,* Mar.-Apr. 1986.

Ward, Gerald M., Thomas M. Sutherland and Jean M. Sutherland, "Animals as an Energy Source in Third World Agriculture." *Science,* May 9, 1980.

Whitney, Charles A., "Generating and Testing Pseudorandom Numbers." *BYTE,* Oct. 1984.

"Who's Afraid of the Big Bad Wolf?" *Forbes,* Nov. 1, 1974.

Wichmann, Brian, and David Hill, "Building a Random-Number Generator," *BYTE,* Mar. 1987.

Other Sources

Beard, Kenneth V., and David B. Johnson, "Raindrop Axial and

Backscatter Ratios Using a Collisional Probability Model." *Geophysical Research Letters,* Jan. 1984.

Bodnarczuk, Mark, "An Operation Approach to High Energy Physics Detectors at Fermilab." Batavia, Ill.: Fermilab, 1985.

Bogert, Dixon, "The Control System for the Fermilab Accelerators." Batavia, Ill.: Fermilab, Aug. 1986.

Courington, Bill, *The UNIX System: A Sun Technical Report.* Mountain View, Calif.: Sun Microsystems, Inc., 1985.

"Design Report for the Fermilab Collider Detector Facility." Batavia, Ill.: Fermilab, 1981.

"Fusion Power." *Information Bulletin.* Princeton, N. J.: Princeton University Plasma Physics Laboratory, 1984.

Henriksen, Georg, "Economic Growth and Ecological Balance: Problems of Development in Turkana." Occasional Paper 11, University of Bergen, Norway, 1974.

Jackson, J. D., ed., *Conceptual Design of the Superconducting Super Collider.* Washington, D.C.: Universities Research Association under contract with the U.S. Department of Energy, Mar. 1986.

Lehner, Francis E., *Theory and Design of Seismographs.* (Technical Bulletin 4.) Pasadena, Calif.: United ElectroDynamics, Inc., no date.

Marsaglia, George, "A Current View of Random Number Generators." Keynote Address, Computer Science and Statistics

16th Symposium on the Interface, Atlanta, Ga., 1984.

Marsh, James G., "Satellite Altimetry." *Reviews of Geophysics and Space Physics,* Apr. 1983.

Quarrie, David R., "The CDF Data Acquisition System." Batavia, Ill.: CDF Computing Group, Fermilab.

Rosenfeld, Samuel, *LINC: The Genesis of a Technological Revolution.* Washington, D.C.: U.S. Department of Health and Human Services, Nov. 30, 1983.

SSC Central Design Group, "Cost Estimate of Initial SSC Experimental Equipment." Washington, D.C.: Universities Research Association for the Department of Energy, June 1986.

Sauthoff, Ned, R. Daniels and J. Bosco, "Tokamak Fusion Test Reactor—CICADA, an Overview." *IEEE* reprint, 1983.

Sauthoff, Ned, R. Daniels and CICADA, "TFTR Control and Data Acquisition." Princeton, N.J.: Princeton University Plasma Physics Laboratory, no date.

"Supercollider Research and Development: The First Two Years." Washington, D.C.: Universities Research Association, Dec. 1985.

"Tokamak Fusion Test Reactor." *Information Bulletin,* Princeton University Plasma Physics Laboratory, May 1986.

"To the Heart of Matter: The Superconducting Super Collider." Washington, D.C.: Universities Research Association, 1987.

Acknowledgments

The index for this book was prepared by Mel Ingber. The editors also wish to thank the following individuals and institutions for their help in the preparation of this volume: **In the United States:** California—La Jolla: Arthur J. Olson, Research Institute of Scripps Clinic; Menlo Park: Rob Cockerham, U.S. Geological Survey; Paul Stoft; Palo Alto: Vernon Andrews, Richard L. Harmon, Hewlett-Packard; Kay Magleby; Pasadena: Bradford Hager, California Institute of Technology; San Francisco: John Backus; Santa Barbara: Peter Malin, University of California; Colorado—Denver: Russell E. Needham, U.S. Geological Survey; Fort Collins: David Swift, Colorado State University; District of Columbia: Robert Ledley, Georgetown University Medical Center; David Lindley, *Nature*; Mary Ann Perozzo, Naval Research Laboratory; Illinois—Batavia: Lawrence Allen, Dixon Bogart, Sergio Connetti, James Freeman, Michael Harrison, Philip Martin, Elliot McCrory, Thomas Nash, Margaret Pearson, Fermilab; Urbana: Kenneth Beard, University of Illinois; Maryland—Gaithersburg: Andrew J. Howard, Genex Corporation; Germantown: Paul Kenney, U.S. Department of Energy; Greenbelt: Shing Fung, James G. Marsh, Goddard Space Flight Center; Massachusetts—Boston: Gwen Bell, The Computer Museum; Cambridge: Joel Moses, John Wade, Massachusetts Institute of Technology; Maynard: Stephen A. Kallis Jr., Digital Equipment Corporation; New Jersey—Princeton: Anthony R. DeMeo Jr., Ned R. Southoff, Princeton University; Short Hills: Brian Kernighan, Kim Pearson, Bell Laboratories; New Mexico—Bob Hutt, U.S. Geological Survey; New York—Yorktown Heights: Susan Eldred, Mary van Deusen, IBM; Oregon—Eugene: Gene Humphreys, University of Oregon; Texas—Dallas: David Yun, Computer Science; Houston: George Phillips, Rice University; Virginia—Reston: Gail Wendt, Rob Wesson, U.S. Geological Survey; Wisconsin—Madison: George Birch, Nicolet.

Picture Credits

The sources for the illustrations that appear in this book are listed below. Credits from left to right are separated by semicolons; from top to bottom by dashes.

Cover-13: Art by Steve Bauer/Bill Burrows Studio. 16, 17: Art by John Drummond(2). 21-27: Art by Al Kettler. 28, 29: Art by Al Kettler; photos by Karl J. Niklas(3); art by Al Kettler(3). 30-35: Art by Steve Bauer/Bill Burrows Studio. 36, 37: Stephen Wagner. 38-49: Art by Steve Bauer/Bill Burrows Studio. 50, 51: Art by John Drummond; art by Steve Bauer/Bill Burrows Studio—photo by Rob Cockerham from USGS. 52, 53: Art by Steve Bauer/Bill Burrows Studio. 54, 55: Art by Steve Bauer/Bill Burrows Studio except waves, by John Drummond. 56-61: Art by Steve Bauer/Bill Burrows Studio. 64, 65: The Computer Museum, Boston(2); courtesy Hewlett-Packard Company; Kay Magleby/Hewlett-Packard Company, bar by Matt McMullen. 66: Courtesy Hewlett-Packard Company(2)—bar by Matt Mc-Mullen—courtesy Hewlett-Packard Company; Digital Equipment Corporation. 68, 69: Art by Steve Bauer/Bill Burrows Studio. 74-77: Art by Peter Sawyer/Design Innovations. 78: Art by Steve Bauer/Bill Burrows Studio. 81-83: Art by Matt McMullen. 84, 85: Art by Matt McMullen; photo by Andrew J. Howard/Genex Corporation— art by Matt McMullen—waves by John Drummond. 86: Art by Matt McMullen. 87: Michael Latil, generated by National Institutes of Health. 88: Michael Latil, generated by National Institutes of Health except art; art by Matt McMullen. 89: Michael Latil, generated by National Institutes of Health. 90: Professor B.W. Matthews/University of Oregon; George Phillips/University of Illinois. 91: © 1985 Arthur J. Olson, Elizabeth D. Getzoff and John A. Tainer/Scripps Clinic and Research Foundation; © 1986 Arthur J. Olson/Scripps Clinic and Research Foundation— © Regents, University of California, courtesy Computer Graphics Laboratory, UCSF. 92, 93: Art by Steve Bauer/Bill Burrows Studio. 96, 97: Kenneth V. Beard. 100, 101: NASA/Goddard Space Flight Center. 107-115: Art by Stephen Wagner. 116, 117: Ellen Cocose, generated by James Freeman/Fermilab.

Index

Time-Life Books Inc.
is a wholly owned subsidiary of
THE TIME INC. BOOK COMPANY

President and Chief Executive Officer: Kelso F. Sutton
President, Time Inc. Books Direct:
Christopher T. Linen

TIME-LIFE BOOKS INC.

EDITOR: George Constable
Director of Design: Louis Klein
Director of Editorial Resources: Phyllis K. Wise
Director of Photography and Research:
John Conrad Weiser

PRESIDENT: John M. Fahey, Jr.
Senior Vice Presidents: Robert M. DeSena,
Paul R. Stewart, Curtis G. Viebranz, Joseph J. Ward
Vice Presidents: Stephen L. Bair, Bonita L.
Boezeman, Mary P. Donohoe, Stephen L. Goldstein,
Juanita T. James, Andrew P. Kaplan, Trevor Lunn,
Susan J. Maruyama, Robert H. Smith
New Product Development: Trevor Lunn, Donia Ann
Steele
Supervisor of Quality Control: James King

PUBLISHER: Joseph J. Ward

Editorial Operations
Production: Celia Beattie
Library: Louise D. Forstall

Computer Composition: Gordon E. Buck (Manager),
Deborah G. Tait, Monika D. Thayer,
Janet Barnes Syring, Lillian Daniels

Correspondents: Elisabeth Kraemer-Singh (Bonn);
Christina Lieberman (New York); Maria Vincenza
Aloisi (Paris); Ann Natanson (Rome). Valuable
assistance was also provided by: Elizabeth Brown
(New York).

Library of Congress Cataloging in Publication Data

Revolution in science / by the editors of Time-Life Books.
    p.   cm.
    Includes bibliographical references.
    1. Research—Data processing.   2. Computers.
I. Time-Life Books.   II. Series.
Q180.55.E4R48 1990   502.85—dc20   90-10884
ISBN 0-8094-7594-4
ISBN 0-8094-7595-2 (lib. bdg.)

For information on and a full description of any of the Time-
Life Books series listed, please call 1-800-621-7026 or write:
Reader Information
Time-Life Customer Service
P.O. Box C-32068
Richmond, Virginia 23261-2068

UNDERSTANDING COMPUTERS

SERIES DIRECTOR: Lee Hassig
Series Administrator: Loretta Britten

Editorial Staff for *Revolution in Science*
Designer: Christopher M. Register
Associate Editors: Jean Crawford (pictures), Peter
Pocock (text)
Researchers: Elisabeth Carpenter, Esther Ferington, Jo
Thomson
Writer: Robert M. S. Somerville
Assistant Designer: Paul M. Graboff
Editorial Assistant: Miriam P. Newton
Copy Coordinator: Vilasini Balakrishnan
Picture Coordinator: Renée DeSandies

Special Contributors: Joseph Alper, William Anderson,
Mark A. Bello, Windsor Chorlton, Martin Mann, John
I. Merritt, Arthur L. Robinson, Don Sider (text); Ann P.
Miller, Carol S. Nicotera, Rachel Weisman (research)

CONSULTANTS

RALPH ARCHULETA is an associate professor of seismology at the University of California, Santa Barbara. He
has done extensive research into the mechanics of earthquakes using computer-modeling techniques.

PAUL CERUZZI, a historian of computer science, is associate curator in the Department of Space Science &
Exploration at the National Air and Space Museum.

GERSON H. COHEN is a research chemist in the laboratory of molecular biology at the National Institute of
Diabetes & Digestive & Kidney Diseases of the National
Institutes of Health. His research focuses on the study of
protein molecules by means of X-ray crystallography.

CARL C. CORRELL, a doctoral candidate at the University
of Michigan, Ann Arbor, is researching the structures of
membrane proteins in the department of biological
chemistry.

ROBERT E. DIEBOLD is a senior physicist at Argonne
National Laboratory. His experimental work involves
high-energy physics with colliding beams of subatomic
particles.

MURDOCK G. D. GILCHRIESE, an associate professor of
physics at Cornell University, is currently working on
experiments for the superconducting supercollider.

ROBERT P. MASSÉ heads the Branch of Global Seismology and Geomagnetism of the U.S. Geological Survey in
Denver, Colorado. He also serves as director of the World
Data Center for Seismology, an international exchange
for seismic data.

KARL J. NIKLAS, an associate professor in the division of
Biological Science at Cornell University, teaches botany
and plant evolution. His research involves mathematical
analyses of plant form and function.

ISABEL LIDA NIRENBERG has dealt with a wide range of
computer applications, from the analysis of data collected by the Pioneer space probes to the matching of children and families for adoption agencies. She works at the
Computer Center at the State University of New York at
Albany.

DAVID F. SUTTER is chief of the Advanced Accelerator
Research and Development Branch of the Office of Energy Research at the U.S. Department of Energy.

REVISIONS STAFF

EDITOR: Lee Hassig

Writer: Esther Ferington
Assistant Designer: Tina Taylor
Copy Coordinator: Anne Farr
Picture Coordinator: Leanne G. Miller

Consultant: Michael R. Williams, a professor of
computer science at the University of Calgary in
Canada, is the author of *A History of Computing
Technology.*